T·H·E
CHILI COOKBOOK

by
Norman Kolpas

Illustrations by
Stephanie Gail Donon

PRICE STERN SLOAN
Los Angeles

Published by HPBooks
a division of Price Stern Sloan, Inc.
11150 Olympic Boulevard
Los Angeles, California 90064
© 1991 Norman Kolpas
Illustrations © 1991 Price Stern Sloan, Inc.
Printed in the United States of America
9 8 7 6 5

Library of Congress Cataloging-in-Publication Data
Kolpas, Norman
    The Chili Cookbook/ Norman Kolpas
       p.   cm.
    Includes index.
    ISBN 1-55788-024-7 (softcover)
    1. Chili con carne. I. Title.
TX749.K595   1991
641. 8'23—dc20   91-3231
                                          CIP

Acknowledgements

My heartiest thanks go to my friends and family who enthusiastically served as taste-testers for this book: Steve and Nicole Berlin; Isabelle, Colette and Bogdan Broniewski; Tim Choy; Peter Goldman; Deborah and Elizabeth Hudgins; Caryn Landau; Linda Peterson; Celina, Francisco, Wendy and Marvin Sanchez; Pam, Bob and Alexandra Sonnenblick; and Julie Mark Tobias. The most valiant testers of all were my wife and son, Katie and Jacob Kolpas, who cheerfully endured the seemingly endless rounds of recipe development.

Thanks go as well to the many chefs and restaurant owners who allowed me to include their own chili recipes in Chapter 5 of this book. They are individually acknowledged with their particular recipes; but they deserve thanks as a group for the contributions they have all made to the furtherance of a classic American dish.

Finally, I would like to thank my editor, Laura Gates, and all her helpful and friendly colleagues at Price Stern Sloan. The actual book you hold in your hands is as much a product of their collective efforts as it is of the author's.

In this book, the spelling *chili* or *chilies* is used for a prepared bowlful of chili. The exception to this rule is in New Mexican recipes, in which case the spelling *chile* is used—this is the traditional spelling in New Mexico for both the peppers and the prepared dish.

Chile or *chiles* refers to chile peppers.

Chile powder refers to ground, dried chiles and the spelling *chili powder* refers to a mixture of spices used for making chili.

Contents

Introduction

Chili is such a well-entrenched element of America's culture and its culinary consciousness that it seems almost redundant to try to define it. Until, that is, you actually start asking people to describe what they consider to be a definitive bowl of chili.

A Texan, staunchly laying claim to the dish for his or her native state, will most likely describe a thick stew of beef liberally flavored with dried red chiles. Press two or more Texans further, however, and the clean simplicity of that definition begins to get a mite fuzzy around the edges, as they begin to debate the merits of including or shunning tomatoes in the recipe, adding cornmeal to thicken the mixture, cooking or serving it with beans, and any number of other fine points that can have a real or imagined effect on the end result.

Geographically broaden the definition beyond that chili-loving state's boundaries, and you allow even more home-grown experts to enter the fray. New Mexicans will tell you to start spelling the dish's name properly—chile with an "e"—and to make it in a way that puts the fresh green or dried red chiles center-stage, where they belong. And as you range farther across and beyond the Southwest, wherever chili lovers are found, you'll find local variations that contribute to an ever-growing roster of "definitive" versions: chilies mild or fiery; chilies thicker or thinner; chilies fine-textured or chunky; chilies with beef, pork, lamb, poultry, game, seafood or simply beans and vegetables; chilies low-down casual or elegantly refined; chilies, in short, of every description.

This book embraces such a far-ranging approach to the dish known as chili, including recipes that match all of the foregoing descriptions. What then, you might ask, do such disparate recipes have in common that allows them to bear the "chili" name? Put simply, they are for the most part main-course, stew-style dishes in which dried or fresh chiles are distinctively present. (Those readers who want to delve further into the Southwestern history of chili—particularly its Texan origins—in delightfully exhaustive detail would be well-advised to seek out a copy of Frank X. Tolbert's masterwork on the topic, *A Bowl of Red.*

On the following pages, you'll find basic information on the ingredients, especially chiles, that give character to a bowl of chili—whatever its origins and however it might stretch the classic definition. The first four recipe chapters are organized by main ingredient, grouping together chilies featuring meats, poultry, seafood and vegetables. Next comes a collection of great chili recipes from leading restaurants and chefs across the country. Finally, you'll find two more chapters that take the pot of chili you cook at home a little bit further—with directions for using chili in other preparations, and recipes for classic accompaniments to chili, from corn bread to margaritas.

Feel free to treat these recipes as a starting point for your own explorations of chili cookery. Learn to stretch that definition yourself, and enjoy the flavorful results!

Shopping for Chili Ingredients

Thanks to the ever-increasing popularity of Southwestern and Tex-Mex cooking, most of the ingredients required to make a decent bowl of chili can be found fairly easily in the modern supermarket—either alongside other, more everyday vegetables and seasonings, or in special "ethnic foods" sections.

Many good-size cities also have Latin American markets where many of these ingredients will be stocked. And you can find a good selection of chiles, both fresh and dried, at many Asian markets.

If you still have trouble locating certain chiles, though, don't be afraid to substitute others—bearing in mind the relative degrees of heat that different fresh and/or dried chiles possess.

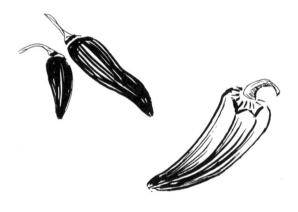

A Guide to Common Chiles & Chili Seasonings

Chiles—whether fresh or dried, whole, chopped, crushed, pureed or powdered—are the very soul of chili. Throughout this book, you'll find chiles used in a number of different forms—sometimes singly, to impose their particular character upon a recipe, and sometimes harmonizing for a more complex layering of spicy flavors.

The following list offers brief guidance to the different kinds of chiles you'll need to prepare the recipes. If you wish to delve into the world of chiles in depth, I can wholeheartedly recommend what is considered the definitive botanical study of the hundreds of members of the Capsicum family, a beautiful and informative book called *Peppers: The Domesticated Capsicums* by Jean Andrews.

A Word of Caution Regarding Chiles

Chiles contain oils that can cause a painful burning sensation upon contact with the eyes or the skin. When working with chiles, fresh or dried, handle them carefully:

• Use kitchen gloves if necessary to protect your hands if you have cuts or abrasions, or if your skin tends to be sensitive.

• Wash your hands liberally with plenty of warm, soapy water after handling chiles.

• Take special care not to touch your eyes after handling chiles. If you do so accidentally, splash plenty of cool water into your eyes to rinse them.

Fresh Chiles

When buying fresh chiles, look for firm-fleshed specimens, with no spots, discolorations or wrinkles. They'll keep best, but still only for a few days, if stored at cool, dry room temperature, loosely wrapped in paper.

Anaheim

Also known as "chile verde" or simply "green chile," this light- to medium-green variety is slender and measures 6 to 8 inches in length. It is generally mild to medium-hot—though some odd specimens may surprise you—and has a slightly sharp, refreshingly astringent taste. I find it to be the best general-purpose fresh chile.

Ancho

Literally "wide," this chile is also known as the "pasilla" or "poblano." It looks like a tapered, triangular bell pepper, 5 to 6 inches long, with medium- to dark-green flesh. This variety is generally a touch hotter and richer in flavor than the Anaheim.

Jalapeño

This dark-green—or very occasionally red—chile measures about 1-1/2 inches long and, with its rounded body and curving stem, fancifully resembles, at least to this author, a toy mouse. Ultra-hot, it has a sharp, distinctive flavor that goes a long way towards flavoring and spicing dishes when used judiciously.

Pasilla

See ancho.

Poblano

See ancho.

Serrano

Slender, straight-sided and measuring 1- to 1-1/2 inches in length, these green or red chiles are very hot, yet also have a certain mellow sweetness to their flavor.

Yellow

Sweet to medium-hot, these 4- to 6-inch, slender, tapered chiles, though usually simply labeled "yellow," may also be sold as "banana peppers" or "Hungarian wax peppers."

Roasting Fresh Chiles

Roasting develops and enriches the flavor of fresh chiles, and is called for in certain recipes.

While several roasting methods exist, the simplest is to spread whole chiles in a shallow baking dish or on a baking sheet with a rim and place in a 400°F (205°C) oven. When the chiles' skins blacken and blister on top, turn them and continue roasting until they are evenly blackened, 20 to 30 minutes.

Remove chiles from oven and cover loosely with a kitchen towel until cool enough to handle. Then peel off blistered skins and pull off stems. Finally, remove seeds and ribs from inside, using a teaspoon if necessary to pick up stray seeds.

Canned Chiles

A number of different kinds of chiles are canned. Sometimes more readily available than fresh chiles, they may be used as substitutes if necessary.

Anaheim

Sometimes simply labeled "green chiles," these are usually roasted, peeled and seeded before canning, and are available whole or chopped. There are several brands available.

Chipotle

These fiery, smoke-dried jalapeños are sometimes canned in a reddish tomato sauce.

Jalapeño

Whole or chopped jalapeños are widely available in cans. They are also sold pickled, which can bring an extra tangy touch to a chili in which they are included.

Dried Chiles

Select dried chiles that look unblemished, unbroken and free of dust or mold. Store them in an airtight plastic bag, away from light, at cool room temperature.

Anaheim

The dried pods of Anaheim chiles that were allowed to ripen until red, this slender, shiny-skinned, 6- to 8-inch pod is generally mild- to medium-hot, with slightly sweet overtones.

Ancho

Dried red pods of the ancho chile, they are less widely available than dried Anaheims.

Arbol

Similar in shape and size to a fresh serrano chile, this dried red variety is fairly fiery.

Chipotle

Light brown in color, this dried form of the ultra-hot jalapeño has a distinctive flavor derived from smoke-drying.

New Mexican

When grown in New Mexico, the Anaheim chile changes its name to the New Mexican chile and is usually hotter in flavor due to the difference in growing conditions.

Pequin

A tiny, round, red chile, no more than 1/2 inch in diameter, this adds incendiary punch when judiciously added to a recipe.

Red Chile Flakes

Commonly available as a bottled spice, these medium-hot flakes of dried chile—seeds and all—add a sharp, medium-hot flavor.

Toasting Dried Chiles

Dried chiles are often toasted in the oven to bring out their flavors.

To toast dried chiles, preheat the oven to 400°F (205°C). Wipe chiles clean with a kitchen towel and spread out on a baking sheet. Place in oven and roast just until their color darkens and their aroma is noticeable, 3 to 5 minutes; watch them carefully, removing them from the oven as soon as they are ready, to prevent burning.

Leave uncovered at room temperature until cool enough to handle, then pull off stems, split open and remove seeds.

Chili Powders

Confusion is a common occurrence when it comes to chili powders. Most spices given this generic label are usually commercial spice blends, as described below. But Latino markets, as well as ethnic foods sections of supermarkets, are increasingly stocking pure ground dried chile powders—literally pulverized dried chiles and nothing else. Each product has its own contribution to make to the chili pot. Whatever kind of dried spice you buy, store it in an airtight container, in a dark, dry place at cool room temperature.

Red (Cayenne) Pepper

A very hot, pure spice made from the dried cayenne chile.

Chili Powder

A commercial spice blend, usually mild to medium-hot, which includes dried chile powder along with such spices as cumin, oregano, coriander, cloves, salt, pepper and other additions.

Paprika

A powdered version of the dried paprika pepper, popular in some European cuisines, and available in sweet, mild and hot strengths. The best kind is Hungarian paprika, followed by Spanish.

Pure Chile Powder

Available in mild, medium-hot (sometimes labeled "ancho") and hot varieties. Usually sold in cellophane bags in ethnic food sections of supermarkets or in Latino markets.

5

Other Common Seasonings

A number of other seasonings commonly find their way into chili. Here are a few of the most frequent contributors.

Cilantro
A fresh herb resembling broad-leafed Italian parsley, with a refreshingly spicy, astringent flavor.

Coriander
Used in the ground form for chilies, this seasoning has an intriguingly sweet spiciness.

Cumin
Almost as integral to chili as chiles themselves, this spice—used as small whole seeds or, more often, ground into a fine powder—has a distinctively pungent, slightly musty flavor.

Oregano
This very popular, aromatic dried herb beautifully complements the flavor of chili—particularly when it includes some form of tomatoes.

A Brief Word on Dried Beans

Cooked dried beans are, to many people, an essential part of or companion to chili. Red beans, pinto beans, kidney beans and black beans are the most common kinds used. But any variety—from great northern beans to navy beans, garbanzos to black-eyed peas, lima beans to lentils—will add its own unique and hearty earthiness to a chili recipe. Feel free to experiment by substituting your favorite kind, or a new variety that appeals to you, in the recipes you find in this book.

Dried beans benefit from a presoaking that helps to soften them. While most packaged beans recommend overnight soaking in cold water, you can hasten the process by quick-soaking the beans—a process employed in many of the recipes in this book. To do this, first sort the beans—taking care to remove any stones or dirt—and rinse them well. Put the beans in a saucepan, cover with cold water and bring to a full boil 5 minutes; then let the pan of beans rest off the heat for an hour before continuing the cooking.

It is also important to note the importance of really boiling the dried beans in any recipe that includes them—for a total of 10 full minutes. This ensures the destruction of lectins—toxins present in dried beans and capable of causing gastric distress.

A Note on Serving Sizes

As you flip through this book, you'll notice that for the most part I give a range of serving sizes for each chili recipe—4 to 6 servings, 6 to 8 servings, and so on. I've presented it this way because, for the life of me, I can't get a consensus on what constitutes a proper-size serving of chili. For some, a good cup is satisfying; for others, 2 or 3 cups isn't enough.

Bearing that in mind, you'll find that generally the lower number yields servings of about 1-1/3 to 1-1/2 cups; the high number, roughly 1 cup of chili. If you know the appetites of your family or guests to be greater or smaller—or if you're planning on making the chili either part of a much larger meal or the sole element of the meal—adjust accordingly.

Cooking Chili for a Crowd

The vast majority of the recipes in this book are tailored to yield portions for a standard family dinner or small dinner party. But chili is also a popular food for entertaining a large, casual gathering, and it's a fairly simple matter to double, triple, quadruple or otherwise increase the number of portions you prepare.

The most important rule to follow when increasing the yield of a recipe is to do your preparatory cooking steps—sautéing of onions, chiles and garlic; browning of meats; pureeing of chiles with broth; and so on—in batches. This will ensure that the job you're doing can be efficiently handled by the home equipment you're most likely using.

Likewise, you might want to consider actually simmering the chili itself in separate, but simultaneous, batches—three separate pots, for example, if you're tripling a recipe. If you're making the chili in one large pot, the cooking time will increase, and you should follow the recipe's visual and taste guidelines for when the chili is done rather than the stated times.

Cooking Times

All cooking times given in this book are, of necessity approximate. They will vary with the kind and size of equipment you use; your own personal assessment of what low, medium and high stovetop heats constitute; and, indeed, the particular ingredients you use.

For example, a chili will reduce to a thick consistency more quickly in a wide, heavy copper saucepan—which retains more heat and has a larger surface area from which liquid can evaporate—than it will in a narrower lightweight aluminum pan. And two identical-looking batches of beans may have vastly different degrees of dryness, requiring shorter or longer cooking times accordingly.

The best guides you have when preparing any recipe are ultimately your own eyes, ears, nose, hands and taste buds. Learn to follow and trust them above everything else, and all your cooking will go more easily and turn out more successfully.

Storing & Freezing Chili

Most of the chilies in this book will keep well for several days if stored in an airtight container in the refrigerator, or for several weeks in the freezer.

Before storing the chili, cool until barely warm, stirring it occasionally to help cool it down. To cool a large pot of chili, place the pot in the sink and surround the pot wiht cold water and ice. Stir the chili occasionally and add additional ice as needed. Never keep chili at room temperature for more than 2 hours. Only when it is cool enough to touch comfortably should you then pack it in storage containers and place it in the refrigerator or freezer.

For freezer storage, either plastic containers with lids or heavy-duty plastic bags are appropriate. Make an extra effort to eliminate excess air from the container before freezing. And label the container with freezer tape or some other appropriate marking system to help you find the chili you want when you want it.

Let frozen chilies defrost overnight in the refrigerator before reheating. Or, if you wish to reheat the chili straight from the freezer, run the container first under hot tap water to loosen the contents; then put the chili in a saucepan with 1/2 inch or so of cold water to help it reheat without scorching.

A Guide to Chili Toppings

With its intensity and richness, a bowl of chili wholeheartedly welcomes all manner of toppings. Try one or more of the following items on your next bowlful, and offer a variety to your dinner guests, allowing them to garnish their own servings to taste.

Cheeses
Cheddar (sharp or mild), shredded or diced
Monterey Jack, shredded or diced
Mozzarella, shredded or diced
Swiss, shredded or diced
Parmesan or Romano, grated
Fresh goat cheese, crumbled or chopped

Dairy Toppings
Sour cream
Plain yogurt
Crème fraîche

Vegetables & Herbs
Onion (white or red), finely chopped
Green onion, thinly sliced
Tomato, coarsely chopped
Tomato salsa (see page 114)
Avocado, cut into small dice
Guacamole (see page 115)
Fresh chopped herbs: cilantro, Italian parsley, chives, oregano, basil, chervil
Dried oregano

Chiles
Fresh mild to medium-hot chiles, finely chopped
Fresh jalapeños, thinly sliced
Pickled jalapeños, thinly sliced
Canned green chiles, chopped
Crushed red chile flakes
Bottled hot chili sauce

Other Embellishments
Croutons, plain or seasoned
Tostaditas (page 109), whole or crumbled
Bacon, cooked crisp and crumbled

MEAT CHILIES

1

There's a simple reason why this is the first and largest recipe chapter of the book: In the minds of most people, chili means meat.

But what a range of choices, flavors and degrees of spiciness in this broad category! There are chilies with beef, veal, pork, lamb and even venison—not to mention combinations of two or more different kinds of meat. You'll find simple, straight-meat chilies; others with meat and dried beans; and still others elaborated with unusual combinations of vegetables and other seasonings. And then, of course, there's a wide choice of heat level—from mildly spiced dishes to chilies that call for tall glasses of cooling drinks to help put out the fire.

As you'll see by flipping through the following recipes, meat chilies have come a long way since the first simple bowlfuls prepared in the old Southwest. Speaking of which, there are several examples of traditional meat chilies here—from old Texas-style versions, to the very basic-yet-delicious chilies of New Mexico, to a recipe that duplicates the neon-orange concoction heaped on chili dogs across the nation.

But there is elegance to be found here as well—in chilies featuring tender sirloin steak, for example, or veal tenderloin with cream, or lamb with black beans. And innovation—in a bean chili oven-baked in the style of old New England.

As food for thought alone, it's a rich and satisfying meal.

Sirloin Steak-Lover's Chili

For those who love a good steak, this is definitely the chili to make. The dish gets extra texture from the fact that it combines both sliced and ground sirloin. While you can certainly buy the two kinds of meat separately, if you have a food processor it's even better to just buy the combined weight in whole sirloin steak; then, at home, slice off a quarter of the total, cut it into rough cubes, and chop it coarsely using the processor's metal blade. If you want to make this moderately spiced chili a little more fiery, include the sliced jalapeño or chopped chipotle in the ingredients list.

10 dried Anaheim chiles, toasted, stemmed and seeded (page 4)
2-1/4 cups beef broth
1/4 cup vegetable oil
1-1/2 pounds beef sirloin steak, trimmed and cut diagonally crosswise into 1/2-inch-thick slices
Salt
Freshly ground black pepper
4 medium-size garlic cloves, finely chopped
1 medium-size red onion, finely chopped
1 fresh jalapeño chile, stemmed, cut crosswise into very thin slices or one canned chipotle chile, finely chopped (optional)

1/2 pound ground beef sirloin steak
1-1/2 tablespoons mild paprika
1 tablespoon medium-hot pure chile powder
2 teaspoons ground cumin
1 (28-oz.) can crushed tomatoes
2 tablespoons brown sugar
1-1/2 tablespoons Worcestershire sauce
2 teaspoons dried leaf oregano
2 teaspoons dried leaf basil
2 teaspoons dried leaf thyme
1 bay leaf
1/3 cup dairy sour cream, for garnish
1/3 cup finely chopped fresh cilantro, for garnish

In a blender or food processor fitted with the metal blade, process dried chiles with 1/2 cup beef broth; set aside. In a large saucepan, heat oil over high heat. Lightly season steak slices with salt and pepper and sear evenly, in batches if necessary, 1 to 2 minutes per side. Set aside. Reduce heat to medium, add garlic, onion and jalapeño chile if desired, and sauté 1 minute. Add ground sirloin and sauté until it loses its pink color, 2 to 3 minutes. Add pureed chile mixture, paprika, chile powder and cumin; sauté 2 to 3 minutes more. Add remaining ingredients, except for garnishes, and simmer until beef is tender and sauce is thick, about 1 hour. Discard bay leaf. Season to taste. Garnish each serving with sour cream and cilantro. Makes 4 to 6 servings.

Beef & Bell Pepper Chili

Diced green bell pepper adds an extra spark of color and flavor to this simple, meaty, medium-hot chili.

1/4 cup vegetable oil
6 medium-size garlic cloves, finely chopped
3 green bell peppers, cut into 1/2-inch
   squares
2 medium-size onions, finely chopped
3 tablespoons medium-hot pure chile powder
1 tablespoon red (cayenne) pepper

2 pounds lean ground beef
1 (28-oz.) can crushed tomatoes
1 cup beer
1/4 cup tomato paste
2 tablespoons dried leaf oregano
1 tablespoon sugar
1/2 tablespoon salt

In a medium-size saucepan, heat oil over medium heat. Add garlic, bell peppers and onions and sauté until onions are transparent, 2 to 3 minutes. Add chile powder and cayenne and sauté 1 minute more. Add beef and sauté, stirring with a wooden spoon to coarsely break up meat, until evenly browned, 7 to 10 minutes. Stir in remaining ingredients and simmer, stirring occasionally, until thick, about 20 minutes. Makes 4 to 6 servings.

Texas Chuckwagon Chili

Chuckwagon cooks were—and still are—great practitioners of the art of making do with little. Out on the range, there was no great wealth of fresh ingredients: You used dried ingredients and other foods that stored well to supplement the fresh beef that was readily at hand. Here's a fair example of the kind of straightforward, no-nonsense, moderate-to-hot chili that might result from that kind of approach. Robust Boiled Beans (page 104) makes a good accompaniment.

12 dried Anaheim chiles, split, stemmed and seeded

4 dried serrano or pequin chiles, stemmed and seeded

2 cups water

1/4 pound chopped suet or lard

6 medium-size garlic cloves, finely chopped

4 medium-size onions, finely chopped

4 pounds beef chuck steak, cut into 3/4-inch cubes

2 tablespoons ground cumin

1-1/2 tablespoons dried leaf oregano

1 tablespoon salt

1/2 tablespoon freshly ground black pepper

3 bay leaves

In a medium-size saucepan, put chiles and water. Bring to a boil, then reduce heat and simmer about 15 minutes. Remove chiles, reserving water. With a large knife, finely chop chiles. In a large pot, heat suet or lard over medium heat. Add garlic and onions and sauté until translucent, 2 to 3 minutes. Add meat and sauté until it loses its pink color, 7 to 10 minutes. Add reserved chiles, cumin, oregano, salt, pepper, bay leaves and half of the reserved chile water. Reduce heat to low, cover and simmer, adding a little chile water only as necessary to keep meat slightly moist, until beef is very tender, about 1-1/2 hours. Discard bay leaves. Makes 8 to 12 servings.

Hot-Off-the-Grill Burger Chili

A vision of a truly great chili burger gave rise to this recipe, in which the meat is charcoal grilled before being combined with the other ingredients. That extra-savory edge of flavor gained by charring the meat goes especially well with the taste of chili powder in this medium-hot bowlful.

2 pounds lean ground beef
Salt
Freshly ground black pepper
3 tablespoons vegetable oil
3 medium-size onions, finely chopped
3 medium-size garlic cloves, finely chopped
1 green bell pepper, finely chopped
1/4 cup chili powder

2 teaspoons sweet paprika
1/2 tablespoon ground cumin
1 teaspoon red (cayenne) pepper
1 (28-oz.) can crushed tomatoes
2 tablespoons tomato paste
1 tablespoon brown sugar
2 teaspoons dried leaf oregano
1/4 teaspoon Tabasco sauce

Preheat the grill or broiler until very hot. Shape beef into 4 hamburger patties, about 1 inch thick, and season with salt and pepper. Grill very close to heat until well-charred on both sides and medium-rare, 3 to 5 minutes per side. Remove from heat and set aside. In a medium-size saucepan, heat oil over medium heat. Add onions, garlic and bell pepper, and sauté until onions are transparent, 2 to 3 minutes. Add chili powder, paprika, cumin and cayenne and sauté 1 minute more. Add hamburgers, breaking them up well with a wooden spoon. Stir in remaining ingredients and simmer briskly, stirring occasionally, until thick, about 20 minutes. Makes 4 to 6 servings.

Beef, Onion, Beer & Coffee Chili

Yes, coffee. A cup of strong, black "joe" adds an extra depth of flavor to this robust but fairly tamely spiced bowlful—already enriched by an abundance of onions cooked until they begin to caramelize. And it gives you the opportunity to challenge your guests with: "Guess what's in this chili besides the beef, onions and chili powder?"

1/4 cup vegetable oil

4 medium-size onions, coarsely chopped

2 teaspoons sugar

4 medium-size garlic cloves, finely chopped

1/4 cup chili powder

1 teaspoon red (cayenne) pepper

1 tablespoon whole cumin seeds

1/2 tablespoon sweet paprika

2 pounds ground beef

1 (12-oz.) bottle beer

1/2 cup strong black coffee

1/2 cup coarsely chopped fresh Italian parsley

2 tablespoons tomato paste

2 bay leaves

In a large saucepan, heat oil over medium-low heat. Add onions and sugar and sauté, stirring frequently, until onions begin to turn caramel-brown, 10 to 15 minutes. Add garlic, chili powder, cayenne, cumin seeds and paprika; sauté 1 minute more. Increase heat to medium, add beef and sauté, stirring to coarsely break up meat, until evenly browned, 5 to 7 minutes. Stir in remaining ingredients, reduce heat to low and simmer, stirring occasionally, until thick, about 20 minutes. Discard bay leaves. Makes 4 to 6 servings.

Chili Dog Chili

The flavor is wonderful. But it's hard to describe the physical properties of a good, classic chili as served on chili dogs without making it sound unappetizing. To help it adhere to sausage and bun, the consistency has to be, well..., sludgy is the most accurate description. And, my wife Katie loves to add, the chili has to have an unearthly neon-orange color "that stains your hands and clothing indelibly"—a byproduct of high proportions of chili powder and tomato paste. This quickly made concoction certainly fulfills those requirements, as well as having a rich, meaty and spicy—but not too hot—flavor that perfectly complements a good hot dog (see Classic Chili Dog, page 94). The combination of beef and pork enhances the flavor, though you can make it with all of one or the other; whatever, use the cheapest ground meat available. The chili is also excellent eaten on its own with cheese and onions but sans frank or bun, or even on spaghetti (page 100). And it freezes well, ready to microwave or rewarm with a little water for an impromptu meal.

1/4 cup vegetable oil
2 medium-size garlic cloves, very finely chopped
1 medium-size onion, very finely chopped
5 tablespoons chili powder
2 teaspoons sugar
1 teaspoon ground cumin

1 pound ground beef
1 pound ground pork
1/4 cup tomato paste
2 cups beef broth
6 tablespoons cornmeal
2 teaspoons salt
2 bay leaves

In a medium-size saucepan, heat oil over medium heat. Add garlic and onion and sauté until light golden, about 8 minutes. Add chili powder, sugar and cumin; sauté, stirring constantly, about 2 minutes more. Add meat and stir and mash with a wooden spoon to break it up into very fine particles, until evenly browned, 5 to 7 minutes. Stir in remaining ingredients, reduce heat to low and simmer, stirring occasionally, until very thick but still slightly fluid, 15 to 20 minutes. Discard bay leaves. Makes 18 to 24 servings on chili dogs, 4 to 6 servings alone.

Quick Beef-&-Bacon Chili & Beans

If you're craving a bowl of homemade chili but just don't have the time for an hour or more of simmering, try this quickly made, fairly tame version.

3 tablespoons vegetable oil
4 medium-size garlic cloves, finely chopped
3 medium-size onions, finely chopped
1 green bell pepper, cut into 1/4-inch dice
1/2 pound streaky bacon, cut crosswise into
   1/2-inch-wide strips
3/4 pound lean ground beef
1 tablespoon chili powder
1 tablespoon red (cayenne) pepper
1 tablespoon ground cumin
1 (28-oz.) can crushed tomatoes

2 (8-3/4-oz.) cans kidney beans, drained
2 tablespoons tomato paste
1 tablespoon brown sugar
1 tablespoon dried leaf oregano
1 teaspoon salt
1 teaspoon freshly ground black pepper
1/4 pound sharp Cheddar cheese, coarsely
   shredded (1 cup), for garnish
1 medium-size red onion, finely chopped, for
   garnish
1/2 cup dairy sour cream, for garnish

In a large saucepan, heat oil over medium heat. Add garlic, onions, bell pepper and bacon, and sauté until onions are translucent and bacon begins to color slightly, 2 to 3 minutes. Add beef and sauté, stirring to break up meat into fine particles, until evenly browned, 7 to 10 minutes. Add chili powder, cayenne and cumin and sauté 1 minute more. Add remaining ingredients, except garnishes, bring to a boil and continue simmering until thick, about 20 minutes. Serve in individual bowls garnished with cheese, onion and sour cream. Makes 4 to 6 servings.

Ropa Vieja-Style Chili

The homey Mexican dish ropa vieja—*literally, "old clothes"—gets its name from the tattered, threadbare look of stewed beef flank. The meat has a wonderfully appealing, chewy texture and a rich flavor that I thought would make a great foundation for a hearty, medium-hot chili. And it does.*

1/4 cup olive oil
2 pounds whole beef flank
Salt
Freshly ground black pepper
4 dried Anaheim chiles, toasted, stemmed
  and seeded (page 4)
4 cups beef broth
2 tablespoons dried leaf oregano
1 tablespoon ground cumin
4 fresh green Anaheim chiles, stemmed,
  seeded and cut lengthwise into thin strips

2 fresh green ancho chiles, stemmed, seeded
  and cut lengthwise into thin strips
1 small fresh jalapeño chile, stemmed, seeded
  and cut lengthwise into thin strips
4 medium-size onions, thinly sliced
4 medium-size garlic cloves, thinly sliced
1 bay leaf
Steamed rice or Spanish Chile Rice
  (page 105), to serve

In a large pot, heat oil over medium-high heat. Season beef flank generously with salt and pepper and brown in oil on both sides, 7 to 10 minutes total. Meanwhile, in a blender or food processor fitted with the metal blade, put dried red chiles, half the broth, oregano and cumin; process until chiles are pureed. Set aside. Remove meat from pot and pour off half the fat. Toss together fresh chiles, onions and garlic and spread half on bottom of pot. Place meat on top and cover with remaining vegetables. Add bay leaf and 1 teaspoon salt. Pour pureed red chile mixture and remaining broth into pot. Bring to a boil, reduce heat and simmer, covered, until meat is very tender, 2 to 2-1/2 hours. Remove meat and vegetables from pot and set aside at room temperature. Meanwhile, increase heat to high and boil liquid in pot until reduced to a thin, syrupy consistency, about 30 minutes. With a pair of forks, pull meat apart into coarse shreds and return to pot with vegetables, stirring to combine well with sauce. Discard bay leaf. Adjust seasoning to taste with salt and pepper. Serve with rice. Makes 4 to 6 servings.

Veal Tenderloin in Chili Cream

Prepared in a classic French manner, this elegant chili includes a subtle—but still noticeable—hint of spice to complement the sweet, mild flavor and tenderness of veal. Serve over steamed rice.

3 tablespoons unsalted butter

2 tablespoons vegetable oil

1-1/2 pounds veal tenderloin, cut into
   2" x 1/2" strips

4 medium-size shallots, finely chopped

2 medium-size garlic cloves, finely chopped

1 green bell pepper, cut into 1/4-inch dice

2 tablespoons mild pure chile powder

2 tablespoons sweet paprika

1-1/2 tablespoons all-purpose flour

1-1/2 cups chicken broth

1 cup half-and-half

1 egg yolk

3/4 teaspoon salt

1/2 teaspoon white pepper

3 tablespoons finely chopped fresh Italian
   parsley, for garnish

3 tablespoons finely chopped fresh chives,
   for garnish

In a medium-size saucepan over medium-high heat, melt butter in oil. Add veal and sauté until evenly browned, 5 to 7 minutes; remove from pan. Reduce heat to medium, add shallots, garlic and bell pepper and sauté until shallots are translucent, 2 to 3 minutes. Stir in chile powder, paprika and flour and cook, stirring constantly, about 1 minute more. Stirring constantly with a wire whisk, gradually add broth and half-and-half. Bring to a boil, stirring occasionally, then reduce heat, add veal and simmer about 10 minutes. In a small bowl, beat egg yolk with whisk until smooth and light yellow. Stirring constantly, slowly pour a ladleful of hot liquid into yolk. Then, stirring constantly, pour yolk mixture into pan. Simmer until thick, about 5 minutes more. Garnish with parsley and chives. Makes 4 to 6 servings.

Albondigas in Green Chili

Savory Mexican-style meatballs, called albondigas, *make this an unusual, and unusually tasty, medium-hot chili.*

3-1/2 cups beef broth

4 corn tortillas, coarsely torn into 1/2-inch pieces

1 pound lean ground beef

1/2 pound ground pork

1 small red onion, finely chopped

1/4 cup finely chopped fresh cilantro

2 teaspoons ground cumin

1-1/2 teaspoons salt

1 teaspoon white pepper

1/2 cup olive oil

4 medium-size garlic cloves, finely chopped

18 fresh green Anaheim chiles, stemmed and finely chopped

4 fresh green ancho chiles, stemmed, seeded and finely chopped

Steamed rice, to serve

In a small saucepan, bring 1/2 cup of the beef broth to a boil. Put tortillas in a medium-size bowl and top with hot broth. When cool enough to handle, add beef, pork, onion, cilantro, cumin and 3/4 teaspoon of the salt and 1/2 teaspoon of the pepper. Mash well with your fingers to combine. In a large skillet, heat oil over medium heat. Moistening your hands with water, form meat mixture into 1-inch balls, dropping them as formed into hot oil and taking care not to overcrowd. Sauté meatballs until evenly browned, about 5 minutes, removing them to drain on paper towels as done. Pour off all but about 3 tablespoons of oil remaining in skillet. Increase heat to medium-high, add garlic and, as soon as it sizzles, add chiles. Sauté 2 to 3 minutes more. Add meatballs, remaining broth, salt and pepper. Bring to a boil, reduce heat and simmer until sauce is fairly thick, 30 to 40 minutes. Serve over steamed rice. Makes 4 to 6 servings.

White Lightnin' Chili

Pale white veal loin and pork tenderloin combine with white beans and green chiles in this mild-looking dish. But don't let its looks fool you: Though it's still within the tolerance range of most people, this chili packs some wallop.

1/2 pound Great Northern beans

1/4 cup olive oil

1 pound pork tenderloin, cut into 1/2-inch cubes

1 pound veal loin, cut into 1/2-inch cubes

4 fresh green Anaheim chiles, stemmed, finely chopped with seeds

4 fresh green serrano chiles, stemmed, seeded and finely chopped

2 fresh jalapeño chiles, stemmed, seeded and finely chopped

2 medium-size garlic cloves, finely chopped

1 medium-size onion, finely chopped

1 tablespoon ground cumin

6 cups chicken broth

1/2 pound tomatillos, coarsely chopped

1 tablespoon dried leaf oregano

1/2 tablespoon dried leaf thyme

1/2 tablespoon salt

1 teaspoon white pepper

1 bay leaf

1/4 cup finely chopped fresh cilantro

1/4 cup finely chopped fresh Italian parsley

In a large saucepan, cover beans with cold water. Bring to a boil over high heat, boil briskly 5 minutes, then remove from heat and let soak 1 hour. Drain and rinse under cold running water. Set beans aside. In saucepan, heat oil over medium heat. Add pork and veal and sauté until evenly browned, 7 to 10 minutes. Remove meat and set aside. Add chiles, garlic and onion to pan and sauté until onion is transparent, 2 to 3 minutes. Add cumin and sauté 1 minute more. Add meat back to pan with drained beans, broth, tomatillos, oregano, thyme, salt, pepper and bay leaf. Bring to a boil, reduce heat and simmer until beans and meat are very tender and chili is thick, about 1-1/2 hours. Discard bay leaf. Before serving, stir in cilantro and parsley. Makes 8 to 10 servings.

Old-Fashioned New Mexican Red Chile with Beef

Natives of New Mexico don't seem to complicate their chiles much more than by spelling the dish with an "e" rather than an "i." That alone acknowledges the fact that the chiles themselves are the star. Indeed, when you say "chile" to a native of the state, you're just as—if not more—likely to be referring to a cooked chile sauce than a main course. Still, by adding or upping the quantity of meat, as in this main-course version of chile colorado, *you get an intensely flavored, very satisfying bowlful.*

20 dried Anaheim chiles, toasted, stemmed
  and seeded (page 4)
4 medium-size garlic cloves, peeled
6 cups beef broth
1/4 cup vegetable oil
2 pounds good-quality stewing beef, cut into
  1" x 1/2" chunks

Salt
Freshly ground black pepper
Steamed rice or Robust Boiled Beans
  (page 104), to serve
1/2 cup dairy sour cream, for garnish
1/4 cup dried leaf oregano, for garnish

In a blender or food processor fitted with the metal blade, put dried chiles, garlic and 2 cups of the broth; process until chiles are pureed. Set aside. In a large pot, heat oil over medium-high heat. Season beef generously with salt and pepper and sauté until evenly browned, about 5 minutes. Pour off half the fat and add pureed chile mixture. Sauté 2 minutes more. Add remaining stock and 1 teaspoon salt. Bring to a boil, reduce heat, partly cover and simmer—stirring occasionally—until meat is tender and sauce is thick, about 1-1/2 hours. Serve over steamed rice or with Robust Boiled Beans, garnished with a dollop of sour cream and a sprinkling of dried oregano. Makes 4 to 6 servings.

Old-Fashioned New Mexican Green Chile with Pork

The same comments I made on Old-Fashioned New Mexican Red Chile with Beef (page 23) go as well for chile verde, which—as the name implies—features fresh green chiles. I find that pork goes excellently with the sharp, slightly astringent quality of the chiles, which gain added finesse by being roasted before they're added to the pot. For the most part, depending of course on the particular chiles you buy, this dish will be no more than moderately spicy.

1/4 cup olive oil
2 pounds boneless pork loin, cut into
    1" x 1/2" chunks
Salt
White pepper
4 medium-size garlic cloves, finely chopped
20 fresh green Anaheim chiles, roasted,
    stemmed, peeled (page 3) and finely
    chopped with seeds

3 cups chicken broth
Steamed rice or Robust Boiled Beans
    (page 104), to serve
1/2 cup finely chopped fresh cilantro, for
    garnish

In a large pot, heat oil over medium-high heat. Season pork generously with salt and pepper and sauté until evenly browned, about 5 minutes. Remove pork from pot and pour off half the fat. Add garlic and, as soon as it sizzles, return pork to pot with chiles, broth and 3/4 teaspoon salt. Bring to a boil, reduce heat, partly cover, and simmer—stirring occasionally to break up chiles— until meat is tender and sauce is thick, about 1 hour. Serve over steamed rice or with Robust Boiled Beans, garnished with a sprinkling of cilantro. Makes 4 to 6 servings.

Pedro Pepper's Pork & Pickled Jalapeño Chili

Having come up with the idea for a chili featuring pork and pickled jalapeños, I couldn't resist fictitiously attributing this fairly fiery dish to Pedro Pepper—a culinary twist on the favorite old tongue twister. You could, in fact, call this recipe a tongue tingler, with the combined tang and fire of canned pickled jalapeños. Serve with white rice and sour cream to cut the fire.

1/4 cup vegetable oil

2 pounds boneless pork loin, trimmed and
    cut into 1/2-inch cubes

Salt

White pepper

4 medium-size garlic cloves, finely chopped

1 medium-size onion, finely chopped

1 tablespoon ground cumin

2 teaspoons ground coriander

2 cups chicken broth

2 pounds tomatillos, coarsely chopped

6 whole pickled jalapeño chiles, stemmed and
    finely chopped

1 tablespoon dried leaf oregano

2 teaspoons dried leaf basil

2 teaspoons dried leaf savory

1 bay leaf

1/3 cup finely chopped fresh cilantro

In a large saucepan, heat oil over high heat. Lightly season pork cubes with salt and pepper and sear evenly, in batches if necessary, 1 to 2 minutes per side. Set aside. Reduce heat to medium, add garlic and onion and sauté 1 minute. Add cumin and coriander; sauté 1 to 2 minutes more. Add remaining ingredients, except cilantro, and simmer until pork is tender and sauce is thick, about 1 hour. Discard bay leaf. Before serving, stir in cilantro and season to taste with salt and pepper. Makes 4 to 6 servings.

Pork-&-Beans-Style Chili with Molasses

Marvelously sweet and spicy—but not too hot—in the same bite, this baked chili was inspired by a New England favorite.

1 pound dried navy beans, soaked overnight in cold water and drained
8 dried Anaheim chiles, toasted, stemmed and seeded (page 4)
3 tablespoons vegetable oil
1 pound lean pork loin, cut into 2" x 1/2" strips
2 medium-size onions, finely chopped
1 medium-size garlic clove, finely chopped
1 fresh jalapeño chile, stemmed, seeded and finely chopped

1/4 pound salt pork, cut into 1/2-inch cubes
6 tablespoons molasses
1/4 cup dark brown sugar
2 tablespoons tomato paste
1 teaspoon ground cumin
1 teaspoon dry mustard
1 teaspoon salt
1 teaspoon white pepper

In a large saucepan, cover beans with cold water. Bring to a boil over high heat, boil briskly 5 minutes and drain, reserving liquid. In a blender or a food processor fitted with the metal blade, puree Anaheim chiles with 1/2 cup of reserved bean liquid; set aside. In a skillet, heat oil over medium-high heat and sauté pork loin strips until evenly browned, 5 to 7 minutes. Remove pork from skillet, reduce heat to medium and add onions, garlic and jalapeño chiles; sauté until onions are translucent, 2 to 3 minutes. In a casserole dish with lid, stir together beans, pork loin, pureed chiles, onion mixture and remaining ingredients, adding enough reserved bean liquid to cover beans; cover casserole. Set oven to 300°F (150°C) and bake until beans are very tender, 3 to 4 hours, adding reserved bean liquid as necessary to keep beans covered. Makes 6 to 8 servings.

Ham & Black-Eyed Pea Chili

There's a special, down-home mystique about black-eyed peas that ties the Southwest and the South in a common culinary bond—as does this straightforward, moderately hot chili.

1 pound dried black-eyed peas
3 tablespoons vegetable oil
2 medium-size onions, finely chopped
1 medium-size garlic clove, finely chopped
1 pound smoked ham, cut into 1/2-inch
    cubes
4 dried pequin chiles, soaked in 1/2 cup hot
    water 30 minutes, water reserved, chiles
    stemmed and finely chopped
2 tablespoons tomato paste

1 tablespoon cider vinegar
2 teaspoons Worcestershire sauce
2 teaspoons brown sugar
1 teaspoon salt
1 teaspoon freshly ground black pepper
1/2 teaspoon Tabasco sauce
3 tablespoons finely chopped fresh Italian
    parsley, for garnish
3 tablespoons finely chopped fresh cilantro,
    for garnish

In a large saucepan, cover black-eyed peas with cold water. Bring to a boil over high heat, boil briskly 5 minutes, then remove from heat and let soak 1 hour. Drain, reserving liquid, and rinse under cold running water. Set aside. In a large saucepan, heat oil over medium heat and sauté onions and garlic until onions are translucent. Add black-eyed peas, ham, chiles, chile soaking water and remaining ingredients, except for parsley and cilantro. Add enough reserved pea soaking liquid to keep peas covered. Bring to a boil and simmer until peas are very tender, about 1 hour, adding more liquid if necessary to keep peas barely covered. Remove about 1/2 cup cooked peas and mash with a fork, then stir them back into pan and simmer 5 minutes more until chili is thick. Serve garnished with parsley and cilantro. Makes 6 to 8 servings.

Hog Heaven Chili

The generous presence of three different kinds of pork inspired this robust chili's name. The seasoning isn't too hot, so the rich flavors of the cured pork still come shining through. Serve with steamed white rice.

5 dried Anaheim chiles, toasted, stemmed
    and seeded (page 4)
2-1/4 cups beef broth
3 tablespoons olive oil
4 medium-size garlic cloves, finely chopped
1 medium-size red onion, finely chopped
1 green bell pepper, cut into 1/4-inch dice
2 tablespoons mild pure chile powder
1 tablespoon ground cumin
1 teaspoon ground cinnamon
1 pound ground pork
1/2 pound fresh pork sausage, casings
    removed

1/2 pound smoked, cured ham, cut into
    1/2-inch cubes
1 (28-oz.) can crushed tomatoes
1 tablespoon tomato paste
1 tablespoon brown sugar
1 tablespoon dried leaf oregano
1 teaspoon dried rosemary
1 teaspoon salt
1 teaspoon white pepper
1/3 cup finely chopped fresh cilantro,
    for garnish

In a blender or food processor fitted with the metal blade, process the dried chiles with 1/4 cup of the beef stock; set aside. In a large saucepan, heat oil over medium heat. Add garlic, onion and bell pepper and sauté until onion is transparent, 2 to 3 minutes. Add chile powder, cumin and cinnamon and sauté 1 to 2 minutes more. Add ground pork and sausage and sauté until they lose their pink color, 3 to 5 minutes. Add pureed chiles and remaining ingredients, except cilantro, and simmer until chili is thick, about 1 hour. Garnish individual servings with cilantro. Makes 4 to 6 servings.

Ground Pork Chili with Ginger & Carrots

This may sound a trifle exotic. Indeed, if I had to try and trace its inspiration, I'd probably arrive somewhere in Asia. But ginger and carrots in a chili actually make a lot of sense: Ginger itself has a fiery side to it, and its sweetness is a natural companion to both pork and carrots. Add the mellow fire of not-too-hot chile powder, and you have a dish of complex and satisfying flavors.

2 tablespoons vegetable oil
3 lean bacon strips, cut crosswise into
   1/4-inch-wide strips
3 medium-size garlic cloves, finely chopped
2 medium-size onions, finely chopped
3 tablespoons medium-hot pure chile powder
1 tablespoon finely chopped gingerroot
2 teaspoons whole cumin seeds
1 teaspoon ground coriander
2 pounds ground pork

1 (14-1/2-oz.) can crushed tomatoes
1 cup beef broth
2 tablespoons tomato paste
2 teaspoons dried leaf oregano
3/4 teaspoon salt
1/2 teaspoon white pepper
2 medium-size carrots, coarsely shredded
1/4 cup finely chopped fresh Italian parsley
1/4 cup finely chopped fresh cilantro

In a large saucepan, heat oil over medium heat. Add bacon, garlic and onions and sauté until onions are translucent, 2 to 3 minutes. Add chile powder, gingerroot, cumin seeds and coriander and sauté 1 minute more. Add pork and sauté, stirring with a wooden spoon to coarsely break up meat, 5 to 7 minutes. Add tomatoes, broth, tomato paste, oregano, salt and pepper. Simmer until fairly thick but still slightly liquid, 15 to 20 minutes. Stir in carrots, parsley and cilantro and simmer about 5 minutes more. Makes 4 to 6 servings.

Mexican Chorizo Chili

A good, spicy Mexican-style chorizo sausage is spicy enough to require minimal additional seasoning for this quick, hearty chili. Cubes of mild white cheese, blended into the chili just before serving, are a nice contrast to the spice.

1 pound chorizo sausage, casings removed
1 pound ground pork
2 medium-size onions, coarsely chopped
2 medium-size garlic cloves, finely chopped
1 green bell pepper, cut into 1/4-inch dice
2 tablespoons chili powder
1 tablespoon dried leaf oregano

1 tablespoon ground cumin
1 teaspoon red (cayenne) pepper
1 (14-1/2-oz.) can crushed tomatoes
2 (8-3/4-oz.) cans kidney beans, drained
1/2 pound fresh Mexican white cheese or Monterey Jack cheese, cut into 1/2-inch cubes

In a medium-size saucepan over medium heat, sauté chorizo, breaking it up with a wooden spoon, just until it begins to render enough fat to coat bottom of pan. Add ground pork, onions, garlic and bell pepper and continue sautéing until meat is evenly browned, 5 to 7 minutes. Pour or spoon off excess fat from pan. Add chili powder, oregano, cumin and cayenne and sauté 1 minute more. Add tomatoes and beans and simmer until chili is thick, 15 to 20 minutes. Stir cubed cheese in and continue simmering until cheese is partially melted, about 1 minute more. Makes 4 to 6 servings.

Sausage & Lima Bean Chili

This oven-baked chili was inspired by a favorite old family casserole served to me by my friend Alice Bandy. But I've taken a lot of liberties with the original concept, substituting fresh Italian sausage and heating up the seasoning considerably—though it's still only moderately spicy. Leftovers keep well for several days if refrigerated in an airtight container.

2 pounds dried small lima beans

1/4 pound streaky bacon, cut crosswise into 1/4-inch strips

2 tablespoons olive oil

2 pounds fresh sweet Italian sausages, casings removed

3 medium-size onions, finely chopped

2 medium-size garlic cloves, finely chopped

3 tablespoons chili powder

1 tablespoon ground cumin

1/2 tablespoon powdered mustard

2 (14-1/2-oz.) cans crushed tomatoes

1/3 cup red wine vinegar

2 tablespoons Worcestershire sauce

1 teaspoon salt

1/2 teaspoon freshly ground black pepper

1 bay leaf

Put beans in a large bowl, cover with water by several inches and soak overnight. Drain well. Put beans and bacon in a large pot and add water to cover. Bring to a boil, reduce heat and simmer until beans are very tender, 1-1/2 to 2 hours. Drain, reserving cooking liquid. In a medium-size saucepan, heat oil over medium heat. Add sausage and sauté, breaking up into coarse chunks with a wooden spoon, until evenly browned, 5 to 7 minutes. Add onions and garlic and sauté until onions are translucent, 2 to 3 minutes. Add chili powder, cumin and mustard and sauté 1 minute more. Stir in tomatoes, vinegar, Worcestershire sauce, salt, pepper, bay leaf and 1-1/2 cups reserved bean liquid. Bring to a boil, then reduce heat and simmer about 30 minutes. Preheat oven to 375°F (190°C). In a shallow baking dish, stir together beans and sauce mixture, adding more reserved bean liquid if necessary to keep beans just covered in sauce. Bake 1 hour, stirring in more bean liquid from time to time if beans begin to look dry. Discard bay leaf. Makes 12 to 16 servings.

Lamb & Black Bean Chili

We've been making this chili—a brainstorm my wife and I shared one lazy Sunday—for several years now. The rich earthiness of the black beans wonderfully complements the lamb. While you can use any inexpensive lamb stew meat, I find it worthwhile to go to the slight extra expense of asking the butcher to cut up some boned leg of lamb: You'll get leaner, less gristly meat that way. I've given a choice of adding less or more chiles to the recipe. We tend to like it on the milder, more subtle side; but it can certainly stand up to a hotter degree of spiciness.

1/4 cup olive oil
1 pound boneless leg of lamb, cut into
   1" x 1/2" chunks
2 to 4 fresh green Anaheim chiles, stemmed,
   seeded and finely chopped
1 to 2 fresh green ancho chiles, stemmed,
   seeded and finely chopped
1 to 2 fresh red serrano chiles, stemmed,
   seeded and finely chopped
2 medium-size garlic cloves, finely chopped
1 medium-size onion, coarsely chopped
1 tablespoon whole cumin seeds
2 medium-size carrots, cut into 1/4-inch dice
1 medium-size red bell pepper, cut into
   1/2-inch squares

1 medium-size green bell pepper, cut into
   1/2-inch squares
3-1/2 cups beef broth
2 (12-ounce) bottles dark beer
1 pound dried black beans
1 pound firm ripe tomatoes, coarsely chopped
1 tablespoon dried leaf oregano
2 teaspoons sugar
1 teaspoon salt
1/2 teaspoon ground white pepper
2 bay leaves
3/4 cup dairy sour cream, for garnish
1/2 cup finely chopped fresh cilantro, for
   garnish
1/2 cup finely chopped fresh chives, for garnish

In a large, heavy pot, heat half of the oil over high heat. Add half of the lamb and sauté until evenly browned, 3 to 5 minutes. With a slotted spoon or metal spatula, remove meat and set aside in a bowl. Repeat with remaining oil and meat. Carefully pour off half the fat from pot and reduce heat to medium. Add chiles, garlic, onion and cumin seeds; sauté, stirring briskly, 1 minute. Add carrots and bell peppers and sauté 2 minutes more. Add broth, beer, beans, tomatoes, oregano, sugar, salt, pepper and bay leaves. Increase heat to high and bring to a boil. Reduce heat to simmer, cover and cook until meat and beans are tender and most of the liquid has been absorbed, 2 to 2-1/2 hours. Discard bay leaves. Garnish individual servings to taste with sour cream, cilantro and chives. Makes 8 to 10 servings.

Ground Lamb & Lentil Chili

Lamb and lentils are wonderfully compatible ingredients, and both go well with the flavor of dried chiles in this satisfyingly robust, not-too-hot dish.

3 tablespoons olive oil
3 medium-size garlic cloves, finely chopped
2 medium-size onions, finely chopped
2 tablespoons medium-hot pure chile powder
1 tablespoon mild paprika
1 teaspoon dried red chile flakes
1 teaspoon red (cayenne) pepper
1 tablespoon ground cumin
1/2 teaspoon ground coriander
1 pound ground lamb

1 cup dried red lentils
2 cups beef broth
1 (14-1/2-oz.) can crushed tomatoes
1 tablespoon dried leaf oregano
1 teaspoon dried rosemary
1 tablespoon salt
2 teaspoons sugar
1 teaspoon freshly ground black pepper
1/3 cup finely chopped cilantro, for garnish

In a medium pot, heat oil over medium heat. Add garlic and onions and sauté until onions are transparent, 2 to 3 minutes. Add chile powder, paprika, chile flakes, cayenne, cumin and coriander; sauté, stirring constantly, about 2 minutes more. Add lamb and stir and mash constantly with a wooden spoon to break it up into very fine particles, until evenly browned, 5 to 7 minutes. Stir in lentils, broth, tomatoes, oregano, rosemary, salt, sugar and pepper; bring to a boil, then reduce heat to low and simmer, stirring occasionally, until lentils are tender and chili is thick, about 30 minutes, adding some water to pot if lentils absorb all liquid before chili is done. Garnish with cilantro before serving. Makes 4 to 6 servings.

Three-Meat Three-Alarm Chili

This is one of the most fiery chilies in the book. But its heat is modified by a richness of flavor from three different kinds of meat—beef, pork and lamb. You'll probably want to accompany it with lots of steamed white rice and ice-cold beer.

10 dried Anaheim chiles, toasted, stemmed and seeded (page 4)
4 dried pequin chiles, toasted, stemmed and seeded (page 4)
2 cups beef broth
6 tablespoons vegetable oil
1-1/2 pounds beef chuck, cut into 1/2-inch cubes
3/4 pound boneless lamb shoulder, cut into 1/2-inch cubes
Salt
Freshly ground black pepper
6 medium-size garlic cloves, finely chopped
3 medium-size red onions, finely chopped

3/4 pound ground pork
2 tablespoons medium-hot pure chile powder
2 tablespoons ground cumin
4 fresh jalapeño chiles, roasted, stemmed and peeled (page 3), finely chopped with seeds
1 (28-oz.) can crushed tomatoes
1 (12-oz.) bottle beer
3 tablespoons tomato paste
2 tablespoons sugar
1-1/2 tablespoons dried leaf oregano
2 teaspoons dried leaf thyme
2 bay leaves
1/2 pound sharp Cheddar cheese, cut into 1/2-inch cubes

In a blender or a food processor fitted with the metal blade, process the dried chiles with 1/2 cup of the beef stock; set aside. In a large saucepan, heat oil over high heat. Lightly season beef and lamb with salt and pepper and sear evenly, in batches if necessary, 3 to 5 minutes per batch. Set aside. Reduce heat to medium, add garlic and onions, and sauté 1 minute. Add ground pork and sauté until it loses its pink color, 3 to 5 minutes. Add pureed red chiles, chile powder and cumin; sauté 2 to 3 minutes more. Add remaining ingredients, except cheese, and simmer until beef and lamb are tender and sauce is thick, about 1 hour. Season with salt and pepper to taste. Stir in cheese and serve. Discard bay leaves. Makes 8 to 10 servings.

Venison & Mushroom Chili

Here's a chili for those who like the robust flavor of game, inspired by my discovery that packages of ground venison from New Zealand were available in local supermarket freezer cases. If your market doesn't have it, a good butcher should be able to fill the order. You can use dried morels or any other kind of dried mushroom that is available; they'll enhance the chili's already rich, moderate-to-hot flavor.

1 ounce dried mushrooms, broken into small pieces
1/2 cup bourbon
3 tablespoons vegetable oil
2 medium-size shallots, finely chopped
1 medium-size garlic clove, finely chopped
1/2 fresh red serrano chile, finely chopped
1-1/2 pounds ground venison
1/4 cup medium-hot pure chile powder
1 tablespoon extra-hot pure chile powder
1 tablespoon ground cumin
2 (12-oz.) bottles dark Mexican beer

1 (14-1/2-oz.) can crushed tomatoes
1 tablespoon salt
1 teaspoon freshly ground black pepper
1 teaspoon dried leaf oregano
1 teaspoon dried leaf basil
1 teaspoon dried leaf thyme
3 tablespoons masa harina
1/4 cup finely chopped fresh cilantro, for garnish
2 tablespoons finely chopped Italian parsley, for garnish

In a small bowl or cup, put mushrooms and add bourbon; set aside to soak. In a large saucepan, heat oil over medium heat. Add shallots, garlic and serrano chile and sauté until shallots are transparent, 2 to 3 minutes. Add venison and sauté until evenly browned, stirring to break up meat, 10 to 15 minutes. Add chile powders and cumin and sauté 2 to 3 minutes more. Remove mushrooms from bourbon and add to pan; strain bourbon through cheesecloth and add to pot as well. Stir in beer, tomatoes, salt, pepper and dried herbs. Bring to a boil, reduce heat and simmer briskly, uncovered, until thick but still slightly liquid, about 1 hour. Sprinkle in masa, stir well and simmer until very thick, 5 to 10 minutes more. Toss together cilantro and parsley and scatter over individual servings to taste. Makes 4 to 6 servings.

POULTRY CHILIES

2

More and more these days, it seems that chilies featuring poultry are all the rage. Popular, casual restaurants proudly offer up bowlfuls featuring ground turkey or chicken, without a trace of meat-based chili on the menu. Duck, enjoying prominence on the circuit of New American Cuisine, also finds its way into the chili bowl, adding its inherent richness to the mellow and fiery flavor of the chile.

You don't have to think long or hard to find an explanation for this trend. Quite simply, Americans are eating more poultry than ever before, aware of the fact that—minus its skin—good old chicken and turkey are remarkably low in the fats that cause so much dietary concern today. What's more, poultry—and particularly turkey—has a richness of flavor that, in chili, can be every bit as satisfying as the taste of red meat.

On the pages that follow, you'll find many a hearty recipe for chili. But you'll also find more mildly spiced dishes that highlight another aspect of our favorite birds—the delicacy of their taste and texture.

So don't be afraid to dig in, eat heartily and know in your heart (and for your heart) that you're doing the right thing.

Chicken Breast Chili Sauté

In its preparation method, this recipe is a cross between a classic French-style chicken sauté and a Chinese stir-fry. The presence of three different kinds of fresh green chiles—one fairly mild, one medium and one hot—more than qualify it as a chili, albeit a fairly nouvelle sort. Mingled with a julienne of red and yellow bell pepper, they give the dish a distinctive—yet fairly subtle—zip. Serve this over a starch to soak up some of the sauce: Spanish Chile Rice (page 105), plain steamed rice or some sort of ribbon-shaped pasta like fettuccine. When we tested this recipe, it was my wife's inspiration to demand mashed potatoes, which went wonderfully with the chili.

1/4 cup olive oil
2 pounds boneless, skinless chicken breasts,
   cut crosswise into 1/2-inch-wide strips
Salt
White pepper
2 medium-size garlic cloves, finely chopped
2 medium-size shallots, finely chopped
2 fresh green serrano chiles, halved,
   stemmed, seeded and cut crosswise into
   thin julienne strips
1 fresh green Anaheim chile, halved,
   stemmed, seeded and cut crosswise into
   thin julienne strips
1 fresh green ancho chile, quartered,
   stemmed, seeded and cut crosswise into
   thin julienne strips

1 medium-size red bell pepper, quartered
   and cut crosswise into 1/4-inch-wide strips
1 medium-size yellow bell pepper, quartered
   and cut crosswise into 1/4-inch-wide strips
3/4 cup chicken broth
3/4 cup dry white wine
1-1/2 pounds firm ripe Roma tomatoes,
   seeded and cut into 1/4-inch dice
2 teaspoons dried leaf oregano
1-1/2 teaspoons dried leaf thyme
1 teaspoon sugar

In a large skillet, heat oil over high heat. Season chicken lightly with salt and white pepper and sauté until evenly golden brown, about 5 minutes. Remove from skillet with a metal spatula or slotted spoon, and pour off all but about 2 tablespoons of oil. Reduce heat to medium and sauté garlic and shallots about 30 seconds. Then add chiles and bell peppers and sauté about 2 minutes more. Add remaining ingredients, along with 3/4 teaspoon each of salt and white pepper; increase heat and bring to a boil. Reduce heat to low, return chicken to skillet and simmer, stirring frequently, until sauce is thick but still slightly liquid, 10 to 12 minutes. Makes 4 to 6 servings.

Great Northern Chicken Chili

Apart from its delicious flavor of chicken breast, white beans and mild fresh green chiles, the surprising thing about this dish is its pleasingly pale, white-on-white color. Great Northern beans are probably the most widely available variety of dried white beans in supermarkets; but you can substitute any other white variety you like. Already-ground chicken breast meat has become increasingly available in meat departments; if you don't see it, ask the butcher to grind up some for you, or buy boneless skinless chicken breasts and grind them yourself in a food processor.

1/2 pound Great Northern beans
1/4 cup olive oil
4 fresh green Anaheim chiles, stemmed,
   coarsely chopped with seeds
2 medium-size garlic cloves, finely chopped
1 medium-size onion, finely chopped
1-1/2 pounds ground chicken breast
5 cups chicken broth
3/4 pound tomatillos, coarsely chopped

1 tablespoon dried leaf oregano
1/2 tablespoon dried leaf basil
1 teaspoon dried leaf thyme
1/2 tablespoon salt
1 teaspoon white pepper
1 bay leaf
1/2 cup finely chopped fresh cilantro,
   for garnish

In a large saucepan, cover beans with cold water. Bring to a boil over high heat, boil briskly 5 minutes, then remove from heat and let soak 1 hour. Drain and rinse under cold running water. Set beans aside. In saucepan, heat oil over medium heat. Add chiles, garlic and onion and sauté until onion is transparent, 2 to 3 minutes. Add chicken and sauté until lightly browned, stirring with wooden spoon to coarsely break up meat, 5 to 7 minutes. Add drained beans, broth, tomatillos, oregano, basil, thyme, salt, pepper and bay leaf. Bring to a boil, reduce heat and simmer, covered, until beans are fairly tender, about 1 hour. Remove cover and spoon out about 1/4 cup of beans; mash them with a spoon and stir back into pan. Continue simmering until chili is thick, about 30 minutes more. Discard bay leaf. Garnish with cilantro. Makes 8 to 10 servings.

Orange & Raisin Chicken Chili

Fresh-squeezed orange juice and golden raisins beguilingly combine with the moderate spice of chili to give this dish a tangy-sweet edge that is especially good accompanied by black beans or white rice and Orange & Red Onion Pico de Gallo (page 115).

1/4 cup olive oil
2 pounds boneless, skinless chicken breasts,
    cut crosswise into 1/2-inch-wide strips
Salt
Freshly ground white pepper
2 medium-size onions, coarsely chopped
2 medium-size garlic cloves, finely chopped
4 fresh green Anaheim chiles, halved,
    stemmed, seeded and cut crosswise into
    thin julienne strips
2 fresh green ancho chiles, quartered,
    stemmed, seeded and cut crosswise into
    thin julienne strips

1 (28-oz.) can whole tomatoes
1 cup orange juice
1/3 cup seedless golden raisins
1 tablespoon dried leaf oregano
1-1/2 teaspoons dried leaf thyme
1 teaspoon sugar
3/4 teaspoon dried rosemary
3/4 teaspoon dried red chile flakes

In a medium-size saucepan, heat oil over high heat. Season chicken lightly with salt and white pepper and sauté until evenly golden brown, about 5 minutes. Remove from skillet with a metal spatula or slotted spoon, and pour off all but about 2 tablespoons of oil. Reduce heat to medium and sauté onions, garlic and chiles until onions are transparent, 3 to 5 minutes. Add tomatoes, breaking them up coarsely with your fingers, and remaining ingredients, along with 3/4 teaspoon each of salt and white pepper; increase heat and bring to a boil. Reduce heat to low, return chicken to skillet and simmer, stirring frequently, until chili is thick, 15 to 20 minutes. Makes 4 to 6 servings.

Tequila Chicken Chili

The distinctive flavor of Mexican tequila, complemented by lime juice, adds an extra dimension of flavor to this unusual chili. Serve with steamed white rice or Spanish Chile Rice (page 105).

3 tablespoons vegetable oil
4 medium-size garlic cloves, finely chopped
2 medium-size onions, finely chopped
1 tablespoon medium-hot pure chile powder
1 tablespoon whole cumin seeds
1 teaspoon dried red chile flakes
1 teaspoon ground coriander
1-1/2 pounds ground chicken
1 (28-oz.) can crushed tomatoes
1/2 cup tequila
1/4 cup lime juice
1/4 cup finely chopped fresh cilantro
1/4 cup finely shredded fresh basil leaves

2 tablespoons tomato paste
1 tablespoon dried leaf oregano
2 teaspoons dried leaf basil
2 teaspoons dried leaf savory
2 teaspoons salt
1 teaspoon white pepper
2 bay leaves
1 tablespoon sugar
2 tablespoons masa harina
Steamed rice, to serve
Fresh cilantro sprigs, for garnish
Fresh lime wedges, for garnish

In a large saucepan, heat oil over medium heat. Add garlic, onions, chile powder, cumin seeds, chile flakes and coriander and sauté 2 to 3 minutes. Add chicken, increase heat to high, and sauté until no longer pink, 7 to 10 minutes, stirring to break meat into rough chunks. Stir in remaining ingredients except masa, rice, cilantro sprigs and lime wedges. Bring to a boil, reduce heat slightly and simmer, stirring occasionally, until mixture is fairly thick but still slightly liquid, about 1-1/4 hours. Sprinkle in masa, stir and simmer until thick, about 15 minutes more. Serve over steamed rice and garnish with cilantro sprigs and lime wedges. Makes 4 to 6 servings.

Quick Leftover Chicken Chili

Instead of making that old tried-and-true chicken salad from your leftovers, try this rapidly simmered chili next time. Served over steamed rice, it's a great weekend lunch dish or busy weeknight supper.

3 tablespoons olive oil
2 medium-size onions, finely chopped
2 medium-size garlic cloves, finely chopped
2 tablespoons chili powder
2 teaspoons ground cumin
1/2 tablespoon red (cayenne) pepper
1-1/2 cups chicken broth
3/4 cup dry white wine
1 tablespoon dried leaf oregano

1/2 tablespoon dried leaf savory
1 teaspoon sugar
3/4 teaspoon salt
1/2 teaspoon white pepper
1 pound leftover chicken meat, torn into 1/2-inch pieces (about 3 cups loosely packed)
1/2 pound tomatoes, seeded and coarsely chopped

In a medium-size saucepan, heat oil over medium heat. Add onions and garlic and sauté until onions are translucent, 2 to 3 minutes. Add chili powder, cumin and cayenne and sauté 1 to 2 minutes more. Add broth, wine, oregano, savory, sugar, salt and pepper. Bring to a boil, then reduce heat to a simmer. Add chicken and tomatoes. Simmer until thick but still slightly liquid, about 15 minutes. Makes 4 to 6 servings.

Hearty Ground Turkey Chili

In recent years, ground turkey has gained wide acceptance as a flavorful and healthier alternative to ground beef. Most any beef-lover would be hard-pressed to tell that there is no red meat in this chili.

2 tablespoons olive oil
2 medium-size onions, finely chopped
2 medium-size garlic cloves, finely chopped
1 tablespoon hot paprika
1 teaspoon dried red chile flakes
1 teaspoon ground cumin
1 teaspoon ground coriander
1 pound ground turkey
1/4 pound mushrooms, coarsely chopped
1 (28-oz.) can crushed tomatoes
1 cup dry red wine
3 tablespoons tomato paste

1 tablespoon dried leaf oregano
2 teaspoons dried leaf basil
2 teaspoons dried leaf savory
1/2 teaspoon dried leaf thyme
2 bay leaves
2 teaspoons salt
1 teaspoon freshly ground black pepper
1 tablespoon sugar
2 tablespoons masa harina
Steamed rice or Robust Boiled Beans
    (page 104), to serve

In a large saucepan, heat oil over medium heat. Add onions, garlic, paprika, chile flakes, cumin and coriander and sauté 2 to 3 minutes. Add turkey and mushrooms, increase heat to high and sauté until turkey is no longer pink, 7 to 10 minutes, stirring to break meat into rough chunks. Stir in remaining ingredients except masa. Bring to a boil, reduce heat slightly and simmer briskly, stirring occasionally, until mixture is fairly thick but still slightly liquid, about 1-1/4 hours. Sprinkle in masa and rice or beans, stir and simmer until thick, about 15 minutes more. Discard bay leaves. Serve over rice or Robust Boiled Beans. Makes 4 to 6 servings.

Mexican Mole-Style Turkey Chili

Mexican mole, *a traditional sauce for turkey enriched with unsweetened chocolate, inspired this rich chili of shredded turkey. The turkey is first stewed with chiles and other aromatic ingredients; then its meat is shredded, and the sauce is finished with a little bitter baking chocolate—the kind available in the baking section of any supermarket. Don't be put off by the idea of adding chocolate to a main course; remember: It isn't sweetened, and acts as an enrichment and subtle flavoring.*

1/4 cup vegetable oil
2-1/2 pounds turkey hind quarters
Salt
Freshly ground black pepper
2 medium-size garlic cloves, finely chopped
1 medium-size onion, finely chopped
2 fresh green Anaheim chiles, stemmed and
  finely chopped
2 yellow chiles, stemmed and finely chopped
4 dried Anaheim chiles, toasted, stemmed
  and seeded (page 4)

2-1/2 cups chicken broth
3 tablespoons dried leaf oregano
1/2 tablespoon ground cinnamon
1/2 tablespoon ground cumin
2 bay leaves
1/4 cup sesame seeds
1 tablespoon sesame oil
1/2 ounce unsweetened baking chocolate
1/2 cup finely chopped fresh cilantro,
  for garnish
Steamed rice, to serve

In a large pot, heat vegetable oil over medium-high heat. Season turkey with salt and pepper and brown evenly on all sides, about 5 minutes. Set turkey aside and pour off half the fat from pot. Add garlic, onion and fresh chiles, and sauté 1 to 2 minutes. Return turkey to pot. In a blender or food processor fitted with the metal blade, put dried chiles, half of the broth, oregano, cinnamon and cumin; process until chiles are pureed. Add to pot with remaining broth and bay leaves. Bring to a boil, reduce heat and simmer, covered, until turkey is very tender, 1-1/2 to 2 hours. Remove turkey from pot and set aside to cool. Meanwhile, boil contents of pot until liquid is reduced by about half, about 15 minutes. Discard bay leaves. When turkey is cool enough to handle, discard skin and bones. With your fingers, tear meat into coarse shreds and return to pot. In a small skillet or saucepan over medium heat, sauté sesame seeds with sesame oil until seeds turn golden, less than 1 minute. Ladle about 1 cup of liquid from pot and pour carefully into skillet with sesame seeds. Add chocolate and stir until it melts. In a blender or food processor, carefully puree sesame-chocolate mixture. Stir into pot. Garnish with cilantro and serve with steamed rice. Makes 4 to 6 servings.

Day-After-Thanksgiving Chili

Here's an alternative to turkey soup, turkey salad or turkey hash. The assumptions behind this delicious, easy-to-make chili is that you've got some leftover turkey meat from Thanksgiving dinner, and that you used a traditional corn bread-based stuffing. But don't wait until the holidays to try it: In our house, we often roast readily available whole turkey breasts for dinner, which yield ample leftovers; and corn bread, a weekend breakfast staple, also provides sufficient extra to go into the chili.

3 tablespoons vegetable oil

3 medium-size garlic cloves, finely chopped

2 medium-size onions, finely chopped

3 tablespoons chili powder

1 tablespoon ground cumin

1 tablespoon red (cayenne) pepper

1/2 tablespoon ground coriander

2-1/2 cups chicken broth

1/2 cup dry white wine

1/4 cup tomato paste

1 tablespoon dried leaf oregano

1/2 tablespoon dried rosemary

1 teaspoon sugar

1 teaspoon salt

3/4 teaspoon white pepper

1 pound leftover turkey meat, torn into 1/2-inch pieces (about 3 cups loosely packed)

1 cup leftover corn bread stuffing, coarsely crumbled, or 1 cup leftover corn bread cut into 1/2-inch cubes and mixed with 1/4 cup extra chicken broth

1/2 pound fresh mushrooms, cut into 1/4-inch-thick slices

2 medium-size green onions, thinly sliced, for garnish

In a medium-size saucepan, heat oil over medium heat. Add garlic and onions and sauté until onions are translucent, 2 to 3 minutes. Add chili powder, cumin, cayenne and coriander and sauté 1 to 2 minutes more. Add broth, wine, tomato paste, oregano, rosemary, sugar, salt and pepper. Bring to a boil, then reduce heat to low. Add turkey, stuffing and mushrooms. Simmer until thick but still slightly liquid, about 15 minutes. Serve garnished with green onions. Makes 4 to 6 servings.

Duck & Red Wine Chili

Duck and red wine are classic companions that happily welcome the spice of chili. For coarsely chopped duck meat, buy the breasts whole from your butcher. At home, cut them into chunks, put in a food processor fitted with the metal blade, and pulse several times until chopped into pea-sized pieces.

2 tablespoons vegetable oil
2 medium-size garlic cloves, finely chopped
2 medium-size onions, finely chopped
2 pounds boneless, skinless duck breasts,
   coarsely chopped
2 tablespoons medium-hot pure chile powder
2 tablespoons sweet paprika
1 tablespoon ground cumin
2 cups dry red wine

1 (14-1/2-oz.) can crushed tomatoes
1 cup chicken broth
1/2 cup finely chopped fresh Italian parsley
1 tablespoon dried leaf oregano
2 teaspoons sugar
3/4 teaspoon salt
1/2 teaspoon white pepper
Steamed rice, to serve

In a large saucepan, heat oil over medium heat. Add garlic and onions and sauté until onions are translucent, 2 to 3 minutes. Add duck and sauté until evenly browned, 5 to 7 minutes. Add chile powder, paprika and cumin and sauté 1 minute more. Add remaining ingredients except rice, bring to a boil, then simmer until thick, 20 to 25 minutes. Serve over steamed rice. Makes 4 to 6 servings.

Cassoulet-Style Braised Duck Chili with Corn Bread Gratin

The classic French dish of baked white beans and meats gets a spicy twist in this Southwestern variation.

1 pound dried navy beans, soaked overnight in cold water and drained
1/4 pound salt pork, left whole
8 dried Anaheim chiles, toasted, stemmed and seeded (page 4)
1 medium-size onion, left whole and stuck with 2 cloves
1 medium-size carrot, left whole
1 medium-size celery stalk, left whole
1 medium-size garlic clove, left whole
1 bay leaf
3 cups beef broth

2 tablespoons vegetable oil
1-1/2 pounds boneless, skinless duck breasts, cut into 3/4-inch chunks
2 medium-size onions, finely chopped
2 medium-size garlic cloves, finely chopped
1/4 cup tomato paste
2 teaspoons salt
1 teaspoon ground cumin
1 teaspoon white pepper
3/4 cup coarse corn bread crumbs
1/2 cup unsalted butter, melted

In a large saucepan, cover beans, salt pork, 2 dried chiles and whole onion, carrot, celery stalk, garlic clove and bay leaf with cold water. Bring to a boil over high heat, boil briskly 5 minutes, then reduce heat and simmer until beans are barely tender, 1-1/2 to 2 hours. Drain, discarding whole vegetables, bay leaf and chiles from pan. In a blender or food processor fitted with the metal blade, puree remaining chiles with 1/2 cup of the broth; set aside. In a large skillet, heat oil over medium-high heat and sauté duck until evenly browned, 5 to 7 minutes. Remove duck from skillet, reduce heat to medium and sauté chopped onions and garlic until onions are translucent, 2 to 3 minutes. In a casserole dish with lid, stir together beans, duck, pureed chiles, onion mixture, tomato paste, salt, cumin, pepper and just enough of remaining broth to keep beans covered; cover casserole. Set oven to 300°F (150°C) and bake until beans are very tender, about 3 hours, adding a little more broth as necessary to keep beans covered. Stir together corn bread crumbs and butter. Uncover casserole and sprinkle crumb mixture over beans, spooning some of casserole liquid over crumbs to moisten. Bake until crust is golden, about 30 minutes more. Makes 8 to 10 servings.

Oriental-Style Duck & Shiitake Mushroom Chili

Far East meets American Southwest in this unusual chili that combines the meatiness of shiitake mushrooms with duck, and the spice of gingerroot with the fire of chiles. It actually makes good culinary sense, considering the popularity of hot chile peppers in certain regions of China, as well as elsewhere in Asia.

12 dried whole shiitake mushrooms

2 tablespoons peanut oil

2 medium-size garlic cloves, finely chopped

2 medium-size shallots, finely chopped

1 fresh red serrano chile, stemmed, seeded and finely chopped

1 teaspoon finely chopped gingerroot

2 pounds boneless, skinless duck breasts, coarsely chopped

1 tablespoon medium-hot pure chile powder

1 tablespoon sweet paprika

1 tablespoon whole cumin seeds

2 cups lager-style beer

1 (14-1/2-oz.) can crushed tomatoes

1 cup chicken broth

1/4 cup finely chopped fresh cilantro

2 tablespoons sweet soy sauce

3/4 teaspoon salt

1/2 teaspoon white pepper

Steamed rice, to serve

In a medium-size bowl, put mushrooms to soak in enough hot water to cover. When soft, after about 15 minutes, remove from water, cut off and discard stems and cut caps into 1/4-inch-wide strips. Set aside. In a large saucepan, heat oil over medium heat. Add garlic, shallots, chile and gingerroot and sauté 2 to 3 minutes. Add duck and sauté until evenly browned, 5 to 7 minutes. Add chile powder, paprika and cumin seeds and sauté 1 minute more. Add remaining ingredients, bring to a boil, then simmer until thick, 20 to 25 minutes. Serve over steamed rice. Makes 4 to 6 servings.

Duck Meatball & Garbanzo Bean Chili

Fresh green chiles and fresh lemon add a wonderful spark of flavor to this unusual chili combining garbanzo beans with meatballs made from ground duck. If you can't get the butcher to grind the duck meat for you, chop it in a food processor fitted with the metal blade.

1 pound dried garbanzo beans

1 pound ground duck meat

2 shallots, finely chopped

2 fresh green ancho chiles, stemmed, seeded and finely chopped

1/2 cup cooked white rice

1/4 cup finely chopped fresh cilantro

2 tablespoons grated lemon zest

1 teaspoon ground cumin

1 teaspoon ground coriander

1-1/2 teaspoons salt

1 teaspoon white pepper

1/2 cup olive oil

4 medium-size garlic cloves, finely chopped

18 fresh green Anaheim chiles, stemmed and finely chopped

4 cups chicken broth

1/4 cup fresh lemon juice

1 lemon, cut into thin wedges, for garnish

In a large saucepan, cover garbanzo beans with cold water. Bring to a boil over high heat, boil briskly 5 minutes, then remove from heat and let soak 1 hour. Drain and rinse under cold running water. Set garbanzo beans aside. In a medium-size bowl, combine duck, shallots, ancho chiles, rice, cilantro, zest, cumin, coriander and 1/2 teaspoon each of the salt and pepper. Mash well with your fingers to combine. In a large skillet, heat oil over medium heat. Moistening your hands with water, form meat mixture into 1-inch balls, dropping them as formed into hot oil and taking care not to overcrowd. Sauté meatballs until evenly browned, about 5 minutes, removing them to drain on paper towels as done. Set aside and, when cool, refrigerate in a covered dish. Pour off all but about 3 tablespoons of oil remaining in skillet. Increase heat to medium-high, add garlic and, as soon as it sizzles, add Anaheim chiles. Sauté 2 to 3 minutes more. Add reserved garbanzo beans, broth and remaining salt and pepper. Bring to a boil, reduce heat and simmer until garbanzo beans are very tender, about 2 hours, adding a little water if garbanzo beans get too dry. Remove about 1 cup of garbanzo beans with liquid and puree in a blender or food processor filled with the metal blade. Stir back into pan and add reserved meatballs and lemon juice. Simmer about 15 minutes more. Serve with lemon wedges for guests to squeeze over individual portions. Makes 6 to 8 servings.

SEAFOOD CHILIES

3

Fish chili?

Yes, the concept gives pause to purists. But some fish are, in fact, hearty enough to make robust chilies. And, in turn, some chiles are sufficiently subtle in their flavors to complement the delicacy of many other kinds of seafood.

Granted, a lighter touch is required here. For the most part, fish does not need, and will not stand up to, the slow simmering characteristic of traditional chilies.

But who says a chili has to cook a long time? The recipes that follow are tailored to the individual requirements of the seafood they feature. Take the Grilled Ahi Tuna Chili, for example, which combines a hearty red chile sauce with the quickly grilled, meaty-flavored fish. Or the swordfish dish, placing chili-marinated and grilled steaks atop a sauce of white beans and green chiles. Or the rapid sautés of fresh chiles with shrimp or scallops.

In the eyes of those who desire strict definitions and rules to govern their culinary lives, these are not chilies in the strictest sense. But to those with open minds and eager taste buds, the recipes that follow are well worthy of the "chili" label.

Grilled Ahi Tuna Chili

In this nouvelle-style presentation, a very basic red chile-and-tomato sauce is prepared using fish broth as a base. Meanwhile, a fillet of ahi tuna—the deep-red, meaty variety—is rubbed with a chili spice blend, quickly grilled, and simmered briefly in the finished sauce to complete its cooking. The result is a simple, elegant dish. Serve over steamed rice.

10 dried Anaheim chiles, toasted, stemmed and seeded (page 4)

3 cups fish broth

6 tablespoons olive oil

4 medium-size shallots, finely chopped

2 medium-size garlic cloves, peeled

1 teaspoon ground cumin

4 medium-size Roma tomatoes, halved, seeded and coarsely chopped

2 teaspoons dried leaf oregano

1 teaspoon dried leaf basil

1 teaspoon sugar

2 teaspoons salt

1 teaspoon white pepper

2 teaspoons mild pure chile powder

1/2 teaspoon ground coriander

1 pound fillet of ahi tuna

Steamed rice, to serve

2 tablespoons finely chopped fresh cilantro, for garnish

2 tablespoons finely chopped fresh chives, for garnish

In a blender or food processor fitted with the metal blade, put dried chiles and 1 cup of the broth; process until chiles are pureed. Set aside. In a saucepan, heat 4 tablespoons of the oil over medium heat and sauté shallots and garlic until transparent, 2 to 3 minutes. Add cumin and sauté about 30 seconds more. Add pureed chiles and sauté about 2 minutes more. Add remaining stock, tomatoes, oregano, basil, sugar, 1 teaspoon of the salt and 1/2 teaspoon of the white pepper. Bring to a boil, reduce heat and simmer until sauce is thick but still slightly liquid, about 20 minutes. Meanwhile, preheat the grill or broiler. Combine chile powder, coriander and remaining salt and pepper. Rub tuna with remaining oil, then sprinkle spice mixture all over it and gently pat spices in. Grill tuna close to heat until well seared, 3 to 5 minutes per side. Cut tuna on the bias into 1/4-inch-thick slices. Put slices in sauce and simmer until tuna is just cooked through, 2 to 3 minutes more. Serve over steamed rice, garnished with sprinklings of cilantro and chives. Makes 4 to 6 servings.

Quick Tuna Chili with Ripe Olives

Chili purists may scoff at the combination. But if you're a real fan of canned tuna, and enjoy it in cooked dishes, this unusual but simple combination is a real eye-opener. Serve it over steamed rice.

3 tablespoons olive oil
3 medium-size garlic cloves, finely chopped
3 fresh green Anaheim chiles, stemmed and finely chopped
1 small onion, finely chopped
1 teaspoon dried red chile flakes
1 (28-oz.) can crushed tomatoes
2 tablespoons tomato paste
1 tablespoon dried leaf oregano
1 tablespoon dried leaf basil

1 teaspoon ground coriander
1 teaspoon sugar
1/2 teaspoon salt
2 (6-1/2-oz.) cans tuna in oil, drained and broken into coarse chunks
1 (3-1/4-oz.) can tuna in oil, drained and broken into coarse chunks
1 cup pitted ripe olives, broken into halves with your fingers
1/3 cup finely chopped fresh cilantro

In a large saucepan, heat oil over medium heat. Add garlic, green chiles, onion and chile flakes. Sauté until onion is translucent, 2 to 3 minutes. Add tomatoes, tomato paste, oregano, basil, coriander, sugar and salt. Increase heat and simmer briskly until thick but still slightly liquid, about 15 minutes. Stir in tuna and olives and simmer until heated through, 2 to 3 minutes more. Just before serving, stir in cilantro. Makes 4 to 6 servings.

Grilled Swordfish, Green Pepper & White Bean Chili

Nouvelle in style, this elegant presentation features briefly marinated grilled swordfish with a quickly prepared sauce of canned white beans and canned green chiles.

3 tablespoons olive oil
2 teaspoons medium-hot pure chile powder
1 teaspoon sweet paprika
6 swordfish fillet steaks, 6 ounces each
1 cup fish broth
1 cup canned, drained Italian-style white
   cannelini beans

2 (4-oz.) cans chopped mild green chiles,
   drained
Salt
White pepper
1/4 cup finely chopped fresh cilantro,
   for garnish

In a large, shallow bowl, stir together oil, chile powder and paprika. In bowl, coat swordfish steaks with oil mixture and marinate. Preheat grill or broiler until very hot. In a blender or food processor fitted with the metal blade, coarsely puree broth and beans. Pour puree into a medium-size saucepan, stir in chopped chiles and warm over medium-low heat. Season sauce to taste with salt and pepper. Season swordfish steaks on both sides with salt and pepper and grill or broil until done but still moist in center, 5 to 7 minutes per side. Ladle sauce into plates. Place grilled swordfish on top and garnish with cilantro. Makes 6 servings.

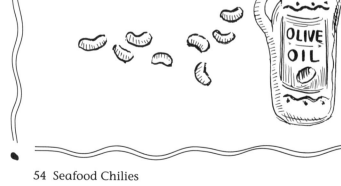

Scampi-Style Shrimp Chili

Fresh green chiles bring a subtle touch of fire to this elegant-but-easy version of classic shrimp scampi. The dish is cooked very quickly; once the ingredients have been prepared, it's ready to serve in under 5 minutes.

6 tablespoons unsalted butter

6 tablespoons olive oil

4 fresh green Anaheim chiles, stemmed, seeded and cut into 1/4-inch dice

4 medium-size garlic cloves, finely chopped

2 medium-size shallots, finely chopped

1 pound medium-size fresh shrimp, shelled and deveined

2 tablespoons finely chopped fresh cilantro

2 tablespoons finely chopped fresh Italian parsley

3/4 teaspoon salt

3/4 teaspoon white pepper

Juice of 1/2 fresh lemon

Steamed rice or Spanish Chile Rice (page 105), to serve

In a large skillet, melt butter in oil over medium heat. Add chiles, garlic and shallots and sauté about 1-1/2 minutes. Add shrimp and sauté until pink and firm, about 1-1/2 minutes more. Stir in cilantro, parsley, salt and pepper; sprinkle with lemon juice. Serve immediately over steamed white rice or Spanish Chile Rice, or with bread to sop up sauce. Makes 4 servings.

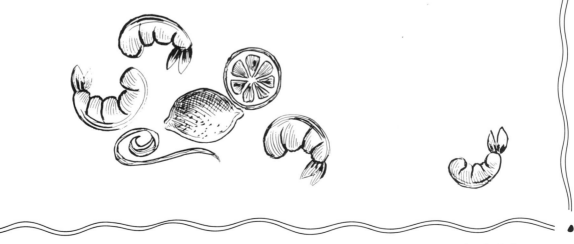

Blackened Shrimp & White Bean Chili

Simple and elegant, this dish presents spicily marinated and quickly sautéed shrimp—an idea borrowed from the Cajun kitchen—atop a bowl of moderately spiced white beans with chiles.

3/4 pound dried Great Northern beans

6 tablespoons olive oil

4 fresh green Anaheim chiles, stemmed, coarsely chopped with seeds

2 fresh red serrano chiles, stemmed, seeded and coarsely chopped

1 fresh jalapeño chile, stemmed, seeded and coarsely chopped

2 medium-size garlic cloves, finely chopped

1 medium-size onion, finely chopped

4 cups fish broth

1/2 pound tomatillos, coarsely chopped

1 tablespoon dried leaf oregano

1/2 tablespoon dried leaf basil

1 teaspoon dried leaf thyme

1 bay leaf

1/2 tablespoon salt

1 teaspoon white pepper

1/4 cup unsalted butter, melted

1 tablespoon medium-hot pure chile powder

1 tablespoon sweet paprika

1-1/2 pounds medium-size fresh shrimp, shelled and deveined

1/2 cup finely chopped fresh cilantro, for garnish

In a large saucepan, cover beans with cold water. Bring to a boil over high heat, boil briskly 5 minutes, then remove from heat and let soak 1 hour. Drain and rinse under cold running water. Set beans aside. In saucepan, heat 4 tablespoons of the oil over medium heat. Add chiles, garlic and onion and sauté until onion is transparent, 2 to 3 minutes. Add drained beans, fish broth, tomatillos, oregano, basil, thyme, bay leaf, salt and pepper. Bring to a boil, reduce heat and simmer, covered, until beans are tender, about 1-1/2 hours, adding a little water if necessary to keep beans barely covered. About 1/2 hour before beans are done, stir together half of the butter with chile powder and paprika. Rub butter mixture evenly over shrimp. When beans are done, heat remaining oil and butter over medium-high heat. When mixture just begins to smoke, add shrimp and sauté until done and slightly blackened, 1-1/2 to 2 minutes. Discard bay leaf and serve beans in shallow soup bowls, topped with shrimp and garnished with cilantro. Makes 4 to 6 servings.

Grilled Lobster Tail & Black Bean Chili

This may well be the most elegant chili you'll find on these pages: a black bean chili, enhanced by fish broth, serving as the dramatic background for medallions of grilled lobster tail.

3/4 pound dried black beans

8 dried Anaheim chiles, toasted, stemmed and seeded (page 4)

4 cups fish broth

4 tablespoons olive oil

4 fresh green ancho chiles, stemmed, seeded and coarsely chopped

4 medium-size shallots, finely chopped

2 medium-size garlic cloves, finely chopped

1 (14-1/2-oz.) can crushed tomatoes

1 tablespoon dried leaf oregano

1/2 tablespoon dried leaf basil

1 teaspoon dried leaf thyme

1 bay leaf

1/2 tablespoon salt

3/4 teaspoon black pepper

4 whole frozen lobster tails, defrosted

1/4 cup unsalted butter, melted

1 tablespoon hot paprika

1 tablespoon sweet paprika

1/3 cup finely chopped fresh chives, for garnish

1/3 cup finely chopped fresh cilantro, for garnish

In a large saucepan, cover beans with cold water. Bring to a boil over high heat, boil briskly 5 minutes, then remove from heat and let soak 1 hour. Drain and rinse under cold running water. Set beans aside. In a blender or food processor fitted with the metal blade, put dried chiles with 1/2 cup of the fish broth. Puree and set aside. In saucepan, heat oil over medium heat. Add fresh chiles, shallots and garlic and sauté until shallots are transparent, 2 to 3 minutes. Add drained beans, remaining fish broth, pureed red chiles, tomatoes, oregano, basil, thyme, bay leaf, salt and pepper. Bring to a boil, reduce heat and simmer, covered, until beans are tender, 1-1/2 to 2 hours, adding a little water if necessary to keep beans barely covered. About 1/2 hour before beans are done, bring a large saucepan of water to a boil and blanch lobster tails in water 5 minutes. Drain tails well, remove shells and membranes and pat dry with paper towels. Cut lobster tails into 3/4-inch-thick medallions. In a shallow dish, coat medallions with melted butter and sprinkle evenly with paprikas. Preheat grill or broiler. When beans are done, grill or broil lobster medallions close to heat just until done, 30 to 45 seconds per side. Discard bay leaf and serve beans in shallow soup bowls, topped with lobster medallions and garnished with chives and cilantro. Makes 4 to 6 servings.

Chilied Crabmeat

In this quick, simple dish, perfect for a luncheon or light dinner course, red chile flakes spice up flaked crabmeat—the kind you can buy ready-cooked at most fish stores or supermarket seafood counters. Alternatively, you could use canned crabmeat. Include more or less chile flakes, depending upon the degree of spiciness you desire.

6 tablespoons unsalted butter
1/4 cup olive oil
1 medium-size garlic clove, finely chopped
1 medium-size shallot, finely chopped
1 to 2 teaspoons dried red chile flakes
1 teaspoon mild paprika
1 pound crabmeat, flaked

1/2 teaspoon salt
1/2 teaspoon white pepper
Steamed rice, to serve
2 tablespoons finely chopped fresh Italian parsley, for garnish
2 tablespoons finely chopped fresh cilantro, for garnish

In a medium-size saucepan or skillet, melt butter in oil over medium-low heat. Add garlic and shallot, and sauté until transparent, 2 to 3 minutes. Add chile flakes and paprika and sauté about 1 minute more. Add crabmeat, salt and pepper, and sauté until heated through, 2 to 3 minutes more. Serve over steamed rice, and garnish with parsley and cilantro. Makes 4 to 6 servings.

Spicy Coquilles St. Jacques

Little bay scallops, no more than about 1/2 inch across, prettily combine with diced sweet and hot peppers in this rapid sauté. Serve on individual plates, surrounded by a ring of steamed white rice to offset the colors—and moderate heat—of the chiles.

3 tablespoons unsalted butter
3 tablespoons olive oil
2 medium-size garlic cloves, finely chopped
2 fresh green Anaheim chiles, stemmed,
    seeded and cut into 1/2-inch squares
2 fresh green ancho chiles, stemmed, seeded
    and cut into 1/2-inch squares

2 red bell peppers, seeded and cut into
    1/2-inch squares
2 pounds bay scallops
1/2 lemon
Salt
White pepper

In a large skillet over medium-high heat, melt butter in oil. Add garlic and, as soon as it siz-zles, add chiles and bell peppers. Sauté 2 to 3 minutes. Add scallops and sauté just until done, 2 to 3 minutes more. Squeeze lemon into skillet and season to taste with salt and pepper. Makes 4 to 6 servings.

Steamed Mussels in Chili Cream

The inspiration for this dish came, in fact, from a Thai meal I had that featured plump mussels in a very spicy chili-and-coconut sauce. I was intrigued by how well the shellfish's distinctive flavor stood up to the heat of the seasoning, and wound up creating this Southwesternized version. If you fear you might not be up to the heat, I've given you the option of using mild, medium-hot or hot chile powder. In any case, serve over plenty of steamed rice to help cool the fire.

2 cups fish broth

1 cup dry white wine

4 medium-size shallots, finely chopped

2 medium-size garlic cloves, finely chopped

6 dozen small fresh mussels in the shell (1-3/4 to 2 pounds), scrubbed and bearded

1/4 cup unsalted butter

1/4 cup mild to hot pure chile powder

3 cups whipping cream

Salt

White pepper

Steamed rice, to serve

1/3 cup finely chopped fresh cilantro, for garnish

In a large pot, bring broth, wine and half of the shallots and garlic to a boil over high heat, then reduce heat until mixture simmers. Add mussels, cover and steam—turning once or twice with a wooden spoon—until shells are all opened, 5 to 7 minutes. Strain steaming liquid through double layer of cheesecloth, and reserve. When mussels are cool enough to handle, shell and discard any unopened ones along with shells; set mussels aside in a covered bowl. In a medium-size saucepan, melt butter over medium heat. Add remaining shallots and garlic and sauté until translucent, 2 to 3 minutes. Add chile powder and sauté 1 minute more. Add cream and reserved liquid, bring to a boil and cook, stirring frequently, until sauce is thick enough to coat a spoon and reduced by about a third, about 10 minutes. Season to taste with salt and pepper. Reduce heat to very low. Add shelled mussels and simmer until warmed through, 1 to 2 minutes. Serve over steamed rice, garnished with chopped cilantro. Makes 4 to 6 servings.

Chilied Oyster Roast

What other appetizer could be at once more elegant and more roll-your-sleeves-up casual than oysters roasted on a charcoal grill? Here, they gain the extra down-home touch of a fresh, medium-hot chile butter that—with the usual latitude allowed by the nouvelle approach to cooking—allows them to join the ranks of seafood chilies.

1/2 pound unsalted butter, softened
1 fresh green ancho chile, stemmed, seeded and cut into 1-inch pieces
1 pickled jalapeño chile, stemmed and seeded

1/4 cup packed fresh cilantro leaves
24 oysters, unshucked and well-scrubbed

Preheat a charcoal grill, or preheat the oven to 375°F (190°C). In a food processor fitted with the metal blade, put butter, chiles and cilantro. Process until well blended. Set aside. Place oysters on hot grill in a single layer, or arrange in single layer on a baking sheet and put in oven. Roast until oysters pop open, 5 to 10 minutes; discard any unopened ones. With tongs, remove oysters from grill or baking sheet to a serving platter. Spoon chile butter over oysters in shells. Makes 4 to 6 servings.

Hot Chili Cioppino

Legend has it that this robust seafood stew evolved around Fisherman's Wharf in San Francisco. A communal effort, it was made from whatever individual contributors would "chip in"—hence the Italianized name. Some cioppinos I've tasted in the past had a spicy edge to them, so it took no great leap of faith to come up with one that is, essentially, a mixed seafood chili. In the spirit of the original, feel free to alter the ingredients, adding whatever kinds of fish you like best or are readily available.

1/2 cup olive oil
6 medium-size garlic cloves, finely chopped
4 medium-size onions, coarsely chopped
4 fresh green Anaheim chiles, stemmed and finely chopped
2 fresh green serrano chiles, stemmed, seeded and finely chopped
2 fresh green ancho chiles, stemmed, seeded and finely chopped
2 green bell peppers, coarsely chopped
1 tablespoon whole fennel seeds
2 teaspoons dried red chile flakes
2 teaspoons ground cumin
2 cups fish broth
1 cup dry white wine

1 (28-oz.) can whole tomatoes
1 (14-1/2-oz.) can crushed tomatoes
1/4 cup tomato paste
2 tablespoons sugar
2 tablespoons dried leaf oregano
1 teaspoon salt
1 teaspoon white pepper
3 bay leaves
1/2 pound firm-fleshed white fish fillet, cut into 1/2-inch pieces
1/2 pound bay scallops
1/2 pound bay shrimp, shelled and deveined
1/2 pound small frozen crab claws, defrosted
1/3 cup coarsely chopped fresh Italian parsley
1/3 cup coarsely chopped fresh cilantro

In a large saucepan, heat oil over medium heat. Add garlic, onions, chiles and bell peppers and sauté until onions are translucent, 2 to 3 minutes. Add fennel seeds, chile flakes and cumin, and sauté 1 minute more. Stir in broth, wine, whole and crushed tomatoes, tomato paste, sugar, oregano, salt, pepper and bay leaves. Bring to a boil, reduce heat and simmer until fairly thick but still slightly liquid, 15 to 20 minutes. Add fish, scallops, shrimp and crab claws, cover and simmer just until cooked, about 5 minutes more. Discard bay leaves and stir in parsley and cilantro before serving. Makes 6 to 8 servings.

VEGETABLE CHILIES

4

It may seem odd, at first, to try to imagine a chili without meat. But, in fact, that perception shifts dramatically when you consider the fact that the dish itself gets its name not from any source of protein but rather from the chile pepper itself.

To be sure, there is plenty of satisfaction to be found in the recipes that follow. Beans and other legumes—among the finest non-meat sources of protein—feature in several of them, providing nutrition and heartiness in abundance. One chili, in fact, showcases seven different kinds of beans—an extravaganza that, though relatively simple to prepare, nevertheless is bound to excite admiration among those to whom you serve it.

There are also several recipes that highlight other vegetables noteworthy for the way in which their tastes and textures have a heartiness every bit as complex and forthright as that of meat. The common mushroom, for example, produces a chili as thick and rich as any you might be tempted to ladle over a hot dog or burger. And a chili featuring chunks of eggplant pleases the appetite especially well, particularly when the vegetable has been chargrilled to give it a smoky edge of flavor.

So dare to be different occasionally when you set out to make chili. Give one of these meatless versions a try.

Mushroom Chili

One thing I've always loved about mushrooms is how meaty their flavor is. Indeed, on their own, they ably stand up to the power of chili powder in this vegetarian recipe that approximates the hearty satisfaction of a meat-eater's dish.

3 tablespoons unsalted butter

3 tablespoons vegetable oil

4 medium-size garlic cloves, finely chopped

4 medium-size shallots, finely chopped

3 tablespoons medium-hot pure chile powder

3 tablespoons mild pure chile powder

1-1/2 tablespoons ground cumin

3 pounds fresh mushrooms, coarsely chopped

1 medium-size green bell pepper, cut into 1/4-inch dice

1 medium-size red bell pepper, cut into 1/4-inch dice

1-1/2 (12-oz.) bottles beer

3 tablespoons tomato paste

2 tablespoons dried leaf oregano

1 tablespoon dried leaf basil

1 tablespoon sugar

1/2 tablespoon salt

1 teaspoon freshly ground black pepper

3 tablespoons yellow cornmeal

In a large saucepan, melt butter in oil over medium heat. Add garlic and shallots and sauté until translucent, 2 to 3 minutes. Add chile powders and cumin and sauté 1 minute more. Add mushrooms, increase heat to high and sauté, stirring constantly, until mushroom liquid evaporates and mushrooms begin to turn golden, about 15 minutes. Add remaining ingredients except cornmeal, increase heat, bring to a boil, then reduce heat and simmer until thick but still slightly liquid, about 10 minutes. Stir in cornmeal and simmer until thick, 5 minutes more. Makes 4 to 6 servings.

Seven-&-Seven Chili

The name of this recipe comes from the fact that it includes seven different kinds of beans and seven different kinds of chiles. It keeps well in the refrigerator or freezer. Take the ingredients list below as mere suggestions, substituting whatever beans and chiles that are available.

1/4 pound (about 1/2 cup) each dried red beans, dried green beans, dried pinto beans, dried kidney beans, dried baby lima beans, dried garbanzo beans and dried black-eyed peas

6 tablespoons olive oil

3 medium-size onions, finely chopped

6 medium-size garlic cloves, finely chopped

1 large fresh green ancho chile, stemmed, seeded and finely chopped

1 large fresh green Anaheim chile, stemmed, seeded and finely chopped

1 fresh red or green jalapeño chile, stemmed, seeded and finely chopped

1 fresh yellow chile, stemmed, seeded and finely chopped

1 dried chile de arbol, toasted in a 400°F (205°C) oven 1 to 2 minutes, stemmed, seeded and coarsely chopped

1 dried Anaheim chile, toasted, stemmed, seeded (page 4) and coarsely chopped

2 tablespoons mild paprika

2 medium-size carrots, cut into 1/4-inch dice

1 medium-size celery stalk, cut into 1/4-inch dice

1 medium-size green bell pepper, cut into 1/4-inch dice

1 medium-size red bell pepper, cut into 1/4-inch dice

2 (28-oz.) cans crushed tomatoes

1 (6-oz.) can tomato paste

4 cups water

1/4 cup sugar

1/4 cup dried leaf oregano

2 tablespoons dried leaf basil

1 tablespoon ground cumin

1 tablespoon dried leaf savory

1/2 tablespoon dried leaf marjoram

1/2 tablespoon dried leaf thyme

1/2 tablespoon ground coriander

1 tablespoon salt

1 teaspoon freshly ground black pepper

1 cup finely chopped fresh cilantro

In a large pot, put beans and enough cold water to cover. Bring to a boil over high heat, boil briskly 5 minutes, then remove from heat and let soak 1 hour. Drain and rinse well. Set beans aside. In pot, heat oil over medium heat. Add onions, garlic, fresh and dried chiles and paprika and sauté 2 to 3 minutes. Add carrots, celery and bell peppers; sauté 2 minutes more. Add remaining ingredients except fresh cilantro. Bring to a boil, reduce heat, cover and simmer until beans are tender and chili is thick, about 2 hours, uncovering pot after first hour. Stir in cilantro just before serving. Makes 16 to 24 servings.

East-of-the-Border Red Bean Chili

The inspiration for this chili is Louisiana's Cajun specialty of red beans and rice. They liberally spice the beans with cayenne and Tabasco sauce; so it's a short leap from them to including more traditional chili seasonings. A smoked ham hock also adds its rich flavor to Cajun red beans; but you have the option of leaving it out if you'd prefer a vegetarian version of the dish. Serve it, of course, over steamed white rice.

1 pound dried red beans
3 tablespoons olive oil
2 medium-size onions, finely chopped
2 medium-size garlic cloves, finely chopped
2 fresh jalapeño chiles, stemmed, seeded and
  finely chopped
1 fresh green Anaheim chile, stemmed and
  finely chopped
1 celery stalk, finely chopped

1 tablespoon ground cumin
6 cups water
1 (14-1/2-oz.) can crushed tomatoes
1/2 cup finely chopped fresh cilantro
1/2 tablespoon salt
3/4 teaspoon white pepper
1/2 teaspoon dried leaf oregano
Steamed rice, to serve
Tabasco sauce

In a medium-size saucepan, put beans and enough cold water to cover. Bring to a boil over high heat, boil briskly 5 minutes, then remove from heat and let soak 1 hour. Drain and rinse well. Set beans aside. In saucepan, heat oil over medium heat. Add onions, garlic, chiles and celery and sauté until onions are transparent, 2 to 3 minutes. Add cumin and sauté 1 minute more. Add beans, the 6 cups water, tomatoes, cilantro, salt, pepper and oregano. Bring to a boil, reduce heat and simmer, stirring occasionally and adding more water if necessary to keep beans covered, until beans are very tender, 2 to 3 hours. Serve over steamed rice, accompanied by Tabasco sauce for guests to add fire to individual servings as desired. Makes 4 to 6 servings.

Variation: Add 1 medium-size smoked ham hock with beans. When beans are done, remove ham hock and shred wih two forks. Return the ham hock shreds to the chili.

Black Bean Chili Primavera

Black beans provide a striking background of flavor, texture and color for an abundance of springtime vegetables in this exciting vegetarian chili.

1/4 cup olive oil
2 fresh green Anaheim chiles, stemmed, seeded and finely chopped
1 fresh green pasilla chile, stemmed, seeded and finely chopped
1 fresh red serrano chile, stemmed, seeded and finely chopped
2 medium-size onions, finely chopped
2 medium-size garlic cloves, coarsely chopped
1 tablespoon whole cumin seeds
1 tablespoon whole caraway seeds
5 cups water
1 pound dried black beans, soaked overnight in cold water and drained
3 medium-size carrots, cut into 1/4-inch dice
2 medium-size red bell peppers, cut into 1/4-inch dice

2 medium-size green bell peppers, cut into 1/4-inch dice
1 medium-size yellow summer squash, cut into 1/4-inch dice
1 medium-size zucchini, cut into 1/4-inch dice
1 pound firm ripe tomatoes, seeded and cut into 1/4-inch dice
1 tablespoon sugar
2 teaspoons dried leaf oregano
1 teaspoon dried leaf basil
1 teaspoon dried leaf savory
1 teaspoon salt
1/2 teaspoon white pepper
2 bay leaves
3/4 cup plain yogurt, for garnish
1/2 cup finely chopped fresh cilantro, for garnish

In a large, heavy pot, heat oil over high heat. Add chiles, onions, garlic, cumin seeds and caraway seeds; sauté, stirring briskly, 1 minute. Add water, beans and half of the carrots, bell peppers, summer squash, zucchini and tomatoes. Stir in sugar, oregano, basil, savory, salt, pepper and bay leaves. Bring to a boil, cover and simmer, stirring occasionally and adding more water if necessary to keep beans covered, until beans are very tender, 1-1/2 to 2 hours. Stir in all but 1 tablespoon each of reserved diced vegetables, and simmer 5 to 10 minutes more, until reserved vegetables are tender-crisp. Adjust seasoning to taste with salt and pepper. Discard bay leaves. Ladle into bowls and garnish with dollops of yogurt and sprinklings of reserved raw diced vegetables and cilantro. Makes 4 to 6 servings.

Sun-Dried Tomato & White Bean Chili

Sun-dried tomatoes have an intensity that is richly satisfying in this meatless chili. If you want to make a lighter version of the dish, seek out dry-packed sun-dried tomatoes and use them instead of the oil-packed variety.

1 pound dried Great Northern beans

3 tablespoons olive oil

4 fresh green Anaheim chiles, stemmed and finely chopped with seeds

1 fresh green ancho chile, stemmed, seeded and finely chopped

1 fresh green serrano chile, stemmed, seeded and finely chopped

3 medium-size garlic cloves, finely chopped

2 medium-size onions, finely chopped

1 tablespoon whole cumin seeds

1 teaspoon red (cayenne) pepper

6 cups water or chicken broth

2 cups packed drained sun-dried tomatoes, coarsely chopped

3/4 cup finely chopped fresh Italian parsley

1-1/2 tablespoons dried leaf oregano

1 teaspoon salt

1/2 teaspoon white pepper

In a medium-size saucepan, put beans and enough cold water to cover. Bring to a boil over high heat, boil briskly 5 minutes, then remove from heat and let soak 1 hour. Drain and rinse well. Set beans aside. In saucepan, heat oil over medium heat. Add chiles, garlic and onions and sauté until onions are transparent, 2 to 3 minutes. Add cumin and cayenne and sauté 1 minute more. Add water or broth, beans, half of the sun-dried tomatoes and parsley, the oregano, salt and pepper. Bring to a boil, reduce heat and simmer, stirring occasionally and adding more water if necessary to keep beans covered, until beans are very tender, 1-1/2 to 2 hours. Stir in remaining tomatoes and parsley and simmer about 10 minutes more. Makes 4 to 6 servings.

Fresh Black-Eyed Pea Chili

When fresh black-eyed peas are in season, this light, flavorful, not-too-spicy dish makes a terrific luncheon main course, served over steamed white rice. If you're a vegetarian, feel free to omit the julienne of ham that adds a touch of extra flavor to the recipe.

3-1/2 pounds fresh black-eyed peas, shelled
4 tablespoons olive oil
2 medium-size garlic cloves, finely chopped
2 medium-size shallots, finely chopped
2 fresh green Anaheim chiles, stemmed, seeded and finely chopped
2 fresh green ancho chiles, stemmed, seeded and finely chopped
1 fresh red serrano chile, stemmed, seeded and finely chopped

3/4 pound Roma tomatoes, halved, seeded and coarsely chopped
1/4 cup finely chopped fresh cilantro
2 tablespoons finely chopped fresh oregano
2 teaspoons sugar
2 teaspoons red wine vinegar
3/4 teaspoon salt
1/2 teaspoon white pepper
Steamed rice, to serve
Fresh cilantro sprigs, for garnish

Bring a large saucepan of water to a boil, add shelled peas and parboil 2 minutes. Drain well, rinse under cold running water and set aside. In a medium-size skillet, heat oil over medium-high heat. Add garlic, shallots and chiles and sauté until shallots are translucent, about 2 minutes. Add reserved peas and remaining ingredients, except for rice and cilantro sprigs. Sauté briskly until peas are tender and chili is thick, about 10 minutes. Serve over rice, garnished with cilantro sprigs. Makes 4 to 6 servings.

Variation: Add 1/4 pound thinly sliced Virginia ham, cut into thin julienne strips, with the reserved peas.

Fresh Green Chile con Queso Fundido

For lovers of fresh-tasting foods, nothing could be simpler: An abundance of fresh green chiles, roasted and then simmered briefly with chunks of fresh white cheese. Anaheim chiles are usually fairly mild, so I've added a few other varieties to spice things up just a bit.

30 fresh green Anaheim chiles, roasted, stemmed and peeled (page 3) and coarsely chopped with seeds, juices reserved

4 fresh green ancho chiles, roasted, stemmed, peeled and seeded (page 3) and coarsely chopped, juices reserved

1 fresh jalapeño chile, roasted, stemmed, peeled and seeded (page 3) and coarsely chopped, juices reserved

3/4 teaspoon salt

1/2 teaspoon white pepper

1-1/2 pounds fresh Mexican-style white cheese or Monterey Jack cheese, cut into 3/4-inch cubes

Robust Boiled Beans (page 104) or steamed rice, to serve

3 firm ripe Roma tomatoes, coarsely chopped, for garnish

1 medium-size red onion, finely chopped, for garnish

In a medium-size saucepan over medium heat, put chopped chiles with reserved juices. When mixture begins to simmer, stir in salt and pepper. Stir in cheese cubes and simmer just until they begin to melt, about 1 minute more. Serve over beans or rice, garnished with chopped tomatoes and onion. Makes 6 to 8 servings.

Chargrilled Eggplant Chili

Chunks of chargrilled eggplant give a satisfying meatiness to this medium-hot vegetarian chili—a distant cousin of the French ratatouille. Serve over steamed white or brown rice.

2 pounds eggplant, cut crosswise into
   1-inch-thick slices
6 tablespoons olive oil
4 fresh green Anaheim chiles, stemmed and
   coarsely chopped with seeds
2 medium-size garlic cloves, finely chopped
2 medium-size onions, finely chopped
3 tablespoons chili powder
2 tablespoons medium-hot pure chile powder
1 pound Roma tomatoes, coarsely chopped

2 medium-size green bell peppers, cut into
   3/4-inch squares
3 tablespoons tomato paste
1 tablespoon dried leaf oregano
1 teaspoon dried leaf thyme
2 teaspoons sugar
1 teaspoon white pepper
Steamed rice, to serve
1/3 cup finely chopped fresh cilantro,
   for garnish.

Preheat the grill or broiler until very hot. Brush eggplant slices on both sides with half of the oil. Grill or broil until charred medium-brown, 3 to 4 minutes per side. Set aside. In a large saucepan, heat remaining oil over medium heat. Add chiles, garlic and onions and sauté until onions are translucent, 2 to 3 minutes. Add chili powder and chile powder and sauté 1 minute more. Add tomatoes, peppers, tomato paste, oregano, thyme, sugar and pepper. Sauté until mixture is thick but still slightly liquid, about 15 minutes. Cut reserved grilled eggplant into 1-inch chunks. Add to chili and cook until tender, 5 to 7 minutes more. Serve over steamed rice, garnished with cilantro. Makes 4 to 6 servings.

GREAT CHEFS' CHILIES

5

Chili has about it the aura of real home cooking—something that can't be bettered outside the realm of your own kitchen. Yet, it's a dish that can also be extraordinarily good when eaten out, as the recipes on the following pages brilliantly demonstrate.

Organized to follow the order of the preceding chapters, the recipes progress from chilies featuring red meats, through poultry, to a robust vegetarian chili and an unusual one featuring both vegetables and fresh melon.

But there's a subtler progression at work here, as well. You'll find terrific versions of chilies that fall well within the category of traditional—including Janos Wilder's tribute in food to early Tucson's legendary town marshall, and the meaty chili chef Arthur Calloway serves up at Detroit's Caucus Club. Then there are chilies that begin to stretch the definition a bit, such as Dallas chef Stephan Pyles' venison chili garnished with goat cheese, and the chili of Muscovy duck served at Eureka, in Los Angeles, by chef Jody Denton. And finally, some of the chilies travel to the cutting edge of contemporary cookery—particularly the grilled rabbit chili from Gethin Thomas, chef of Adirondacks in Washington, D.C., and John Sedlar's dish of green chili with melon, developed at his Santa Monica restaurant, Bikini.

And, as the geographic range of these chefs succinctly demonstrates, there's one more important lesson to be learned here: Good chili knows no boundaries.

Venison Chili with Texas Goat Cheese & Blue Corn Skillet Sticks

Stephan Pyles, Routh Street Cafe & Baby Routh, Dallas, Texas

At his two very popular Dallas restaurants, native Texan Stephan Pyles combines a love of his state's traditional ingredients with the technique and finesse he gained in some of France's finest kitchens. That dynamic combination is well evident in this flavorful chili, which he garnishes with goat cheese and accompanies with blue corn bread sticks. If you have trouble hunting down goat cheese from Texas, substitute whatever fresh creamy variety is available locally; and use yellow cornmeal if blue isn't available.

1/2 cup vegetable oil
2 pounds venison, well-trimmed and coarsely chopped
6 garlic cloves, finely chopped
1 onion, coarsely chopped
1/4 cup pureed roasted ancho chile (see page 3)

1 tablespoon pureed roasted chipotle chile (see page 3)
4 medium-size tomatoes, coarsely chopped
1/2 teaspoon ground cumin
1 quart light veal stock, or water
Salt and freshly ground black pepper
1/4 pound Texas goat cheese, for garnish

In a heavy saucepan, heat oil over medium heat. Add venison, garlic and onion; sauté until meat is evenly browned, 5 to 7 minutes. Stir in chile purees, tomatoes and cumin; cook 15 minutes more, stirring frequently. Add stock and bring to a boil; reduce heat and simmer 1-1/2 hours, stirring occasionally. Season to taste with salt and black pepper. Ladle into bowls and garnish with goat cheese. Accompany with Blue Corn Skillet Sticks (opposite). Makes 6 servings.

Note: Chiles are first roasted, then pureed in this recipe.

Blue Corn Skillet Sticks

1-1/4 cups blue cornmeal
1 cup all-purpose flour
2 tablespoons sugar
1 teaspoon salt
1 teaspoon baking powder
2 tablespoons unsalted butter or vegetable oil
3 serrano chiles, stemmed, seeded and finely
    chopped
3 garlic cloves, finely chopped

2 eggs
6 tablespoons shortening, melted and cooled
6 tablespoons unsalted butter, melted and
    cooled
1 cup buttermilk, at room temperature
1/4 teaspoon baking soda
3 tablespoons finely chopped fresh cilantro

Preheat oven to 400°F (205°C). Lightly grease cast-iron corn stick pans or muffin pans. In a medium-size bowl, sift together cornmeal, flour, sugar, salt and baking powder. Set aside. In a small skillet, heat butter or oil over medium heat and sauté chiles and garlic 1 to 2 minutes. Set aside. In another bowl, lightly beat eggs, then stir in melted shortening and butter. Stir together buttermilk and baking soda and stir into egg mixture. Pour liquid mixture over dry ingredients and beat just until smooth; do not over mix. Fold in chiles, garlic and cilantro. Pour batter into prepared baking pans. Bake in center of oven until golden brown, 18 to 20 minutes. Makes 24 corn sticks or 12 muffins.

Marshall Duffield's Smokin' Pistol Bowl o' Red

Janos Wilder, Janos Restaurant, Tucson, Arizona

"Tucson in the 1860s was a rugged frontier town where the most powerful were usually the strongest and the accuracy of the pistol enforced the rule of law," says Janos Wilder, one of the modern city's most innovative chefs. "The marshall at the time was Milton Duffield, who got and held his job due to his fearlessness, fighting ability and good aim. Marshall Duffield lived in part of the historic adobe home which is now Janos Restaurant, and stories of his courage and ruthlessness are often told to guests as they tour the magnificent old structure after dinner. One of my favorites comes from an account in the local paper, which quotes Duffield after a particularly harrowing night when he was attacked in his sleep by two knife-wielding banditos: 'I would have shot them,' he said. 'But when I went to cock my pistol, I noticed my thumb was gone.' This chili recipe is for Marshall Duffield."

1 pound medium-hot chorizo, casing
  removed
2 large onions, finely chopped
3 pounds fresh pork butt, trimmed and cut
  into large dice
10 to 12 medium-size garlic cloves, finely
  chopped (4 tablespoons)
3 Mesquite-Smoked Anaheim Chiles, see
  opposite, cut into medium-size dice
2 Mesquite-Smoked Poblano Chiles, see
  opposite, cut into medium-size dice
6 tablespoons good-quality chili powder
1 tablespoon ground cumin
Salt

Freshly ground black pepper
1-1/2 to 2 quarts veal stock
3 cups cooked black beans
2 cups fresh corn kernels
1-1/2 pounds Roma tomatoes, cut into
  medium-size dice
6 tablespoons fresh lime juice
1 pound queso blanco (Mexican-style fresh
  white cheese), crumbled or coarsely
  shredded, for garnish
1 cup Fresh Tomato Salsa (page 114),
  for garnish
1 cup finely chopped fresh cilantro,
  for garnish

In a large pot over medium heat, sauté chorizo and onions until onions are translucent and grease is completely rendered from chorizo, 5 to 7 minutes. Drain off and discard all grease. Add pork butt, garlic, smoked chiles, chili powder, cumin, salt and pepper to taste; increase heat to high and sauté until pork is lightly browned, 5 to 7 minutes. Add enough veal stock to cover; bring to a boil, then reduce heat and simmer until pork is tender, about 1 hour. Add beans, corn and diced tomatoes and simmer 5 minutes. Stir in lime juice and serve, garnishing each bowl with queso blanco, salsa and cilantro. Makes 12 servings.

Mesquite-Smoked Chiles

To make a simple smoker, put a small barbecue or a large, heavy old pot in a clear area outdoors and light and burn charcoal briquets in it. While coals are heating, soak a handful of mesquite chips in cold water, and roast, peel and seed chiles (see page 3). When coals have almost completely burned down but are still hot, drain mesquite chips well and scatter over coals; spray with water if they catch fire. Set a fine-mesh metal rack at least 8 inches above chips. Place roasted peppers on rack, cover loosely with a pot lid and smoke 5 minutes. Remove peppers and let cool before using in recipe.

Doc Martin's Award-Winning Green Chile

Doc Martin's Restaurant at The Historic Taos Inn, Taos, New Mexico

One of the finest places to sleep or dine in Taos is The Historic Taos Inn, a charming hostelry—on the National and State Registers of Historic Places—made up of several adjoining houses dating from the 1800s. The first of those to be so converted was, around the turn of the century, home to the town's first physician, Dr. Thomas Paul Martin, whose widow, Helen, opened it as the Hotel Martin in 1936. Today, Dr. Martin's house is the site of the inn's outstanding restaurant, where I once ate a truly memorable bowl of New Mexican green chile (spelled, in local style, with an "e" and not an "i"), the recipe for which hotel owner Carolyn Haddock kindly agreed to share. She says the chile is best reheated, and suggests garnishing it with shredded cheese, shredded lettuce and diced tomatoes, and accompanying it with Honey-Cinnamon Sopaipillas (page 110) and ice-cold beer.

7 tablespoons unsalted butter

6 tablespoons all-purpose flour

1/4 cup vegetable oil

1/2 pound ground beef

1/2 pound ground pork

1/2 pound leftover roast beef, cut into
   1/2-inch cubes

1 medium-size onion, finely chopped

1 medium-size garlic clove, finely chopped

1/2 cup finely chopped fresh cilantro

2 teaspoons dried minced garlic

2 teaspoons ground cumin

2 teaspoons Tabasco sauce

1 teaspoon dried leaf oregano

1 teaspoon dried leaf parsley

1 teaspoon onion powder

1/2 teaspoon freshly ground black pepper

3 cups chicken or beef broth

1 (12-ounce) bottle Mexican beer

2 pounds fresh green New Mexican or
   Anaheim chiles, roasted (page 3),
   stemmed, peeled, seeded and coarsely
   chopped

1 large tomato, coarsely chopped

In a small saucepan or skillet over low heat, melt 4 tablespoons of the butter; stir in 4 tablespoons of the flour and cook, stirring constantly, about 1 minute, to make a smooth paste or roux. Set aside. In a large saucepan, heat oil over medium-high heat; add beef, pork and roast beef and sauté until evenly browned, 5 to 7 minutes. In a separate saucepan, melt remaining butter over medium heat and sauté onion and garlic until translucent, 3 to 5 minutes. Add onion and garlic to meat, and add remaining flour, cilantro, granulated garlic, cumin, Tabasco sauce, oregano, parsley, onion powder and pepper. Stir over low heat 2 to 3 minutes. Add broth, beer, green chiles and tomato; bring to a simmer. Stir in reserved roux. Simmer gently 45 minutes to 1 hour. Makes 6 to 8 servings.

Chicken "Chili" Tacos

Dean Fearing, The Mansion on Turtle Creek, Dallas, Texas

The restaurant at Dallas' most luxurious hotel features the cuisine of a chef who artfully, guilelessly combines classical finesse with down-home good cookin'. Dean Fearing's version of chili rolls up a cheese-enriched chicken breast mixture in warm flour tortillas—a marriage of vivid flavors and the kind of casual presentation that encourages guests to roll up their sleeves and dig in.

1/3 cup olive oil
5 whole boneless skinless chicken breasts, cut into 3/4-inch cubes
3 large onions, cut into 1/2-inch squares
3 large bell peppers, cut into 1/2-inch squares
3 large tomatoes, seeded and cut into 1/2-inch cubes
3 fresh jalapeño chiles, stemmed and finely chopped with seeds
3 large garlic cloves, finely chopped
1 cup chicken broth

1/4 cup finely chopped fresh cilantro
2 teaspoons ground cumin
2 teaspoons ground coriander
1/2 tablespoon chili powder
3 cups shredded Monterey Jack cheese (12 ounces)
Fresh lime juice
Salt
24 flour tortillas
Guacamole, salsa, sour cream, sliced jalapeños, sliced ripe olives, for garnish

Heat a large skillet over medium-high heat. Add oil and sauté chicken until lightly browned, about 3 minutes. Add onions and bell peppers and sauté until onions are translucent, 2 to 3 minutes. Add tomatoes, jalapeños, garlic, broth, cilantro, cumin, coriander and chili powder. Bring to a boil, then reduce heat and simmer 20 minutes. Preheat oven to 350°F (175°C) and put tortillas in about 5 minutes before chicken is done. Sprinkle cheese into chicken mixture, stirring until thoroughly melted. Serve, letting each guest spoon chicken/cheese mixture into tortillas to be rolled up and garnished to taste. Makes 12 servings.

Maxwell's Plum Chili

Warner LeRoy, Tavern on the Green, New York, New York

In the early 1970s, I ate an extraordinarily good bowl of chili at Maxwell's Plum restaurant in Manhattan. Alas, neither the New York nor the San Francisco Maxwell's survives today, though owner Warner LeRoy's grand hospitality continues at the Tavern on the Green. And his office kindly dug from their files for me a copy of their master recipe for that meaty, tangy, not-too-hot bowlful I remember after all these years.

6 dried Anaheim chiles, stemmed and seeded
3/4 cup water
1 tablespoon dried leaf oregano
1/2 cup beer
2 cups fat from rendered beef suet
3 pounds beef round steak, cut into
   1/2-inch chunks
3 pounds beef chuck, cut into
   1/2-inch chunks
6 medium-size garlic cloves, finely chopped
1/2 cup chili powder
3 tablespoons Spanish paprika
3 tablespoons ground cumin

3 medium-size onions, finely chopped
2 tablespoons cider vinegar
4 cups beef broth
1 cup stewed tomatoes, pureed
2 cups rich beef stock
2 tablespoons masa harina
Garlic powder (optional)
Chili Beans (opposite)
3/4 pound Cheddar cheese, shredded
   (12 cups), for garnish
4 medium-size onions, finely chopped, for
   garnish
2-1/2 cups dairy sour cream, for garnish

In a small saucepan, put chiles and water. Bring to a boil, then simmer 30 minutes; remove from heat and set aside. In a small bowl, stir oregano into beer and leave to steep like tea. In a large pot, melt suet over medium-high heat. Season beef chunks with pepper to taste and sauté in suet until evenly browned, 10 to 15 minutes. Drain well and return meat to pot. Add garlic, chili powder, paprika and cumin and cook over low heat, covered, adding just enough water drained from soaking chiles to moisten meat, slightly, about 40 minutes. Peel skins from boiled chiles. With a fork, mash chile pulp and add to meat with onions, vinegar, beef broth, pureed tomatoes and half of the stock. Simmer gently, covered, 45 minutes. Stir masa into remaining stock and stir into pot; simmer 45 minutes more. Taste for seasoning, adding more salt, chili powder, dried oregano or garlic powder to taste if necessary. Ladle chili into individual bowls and place on wooden planks with smaller bowls of Chili Beans and small containers of cheese, chopped onions and sour cream for guests to use as garnishes. Makes 12 servings.

Chili Beans

1 pound dried red beans	1/2 head garlic
1 medium-size onion	1/4 pound slab bacon
2 whole cloves	Salt
2 bay leaves	White pepper

The night before serving, put beans in a large bowl and add cold water to cover by several inches; soak overnight. Drain well. In a large pot, put soaked beans, onion studded with whole cloves, bay leaves, garlic and bacon; add 2 quarts water. Bring to a boil, reduce heat and simmer until beans are tender, about 1-3/4 hours. Season to taste with salt and white pepper. Discard onion, bay leaves and bacon.

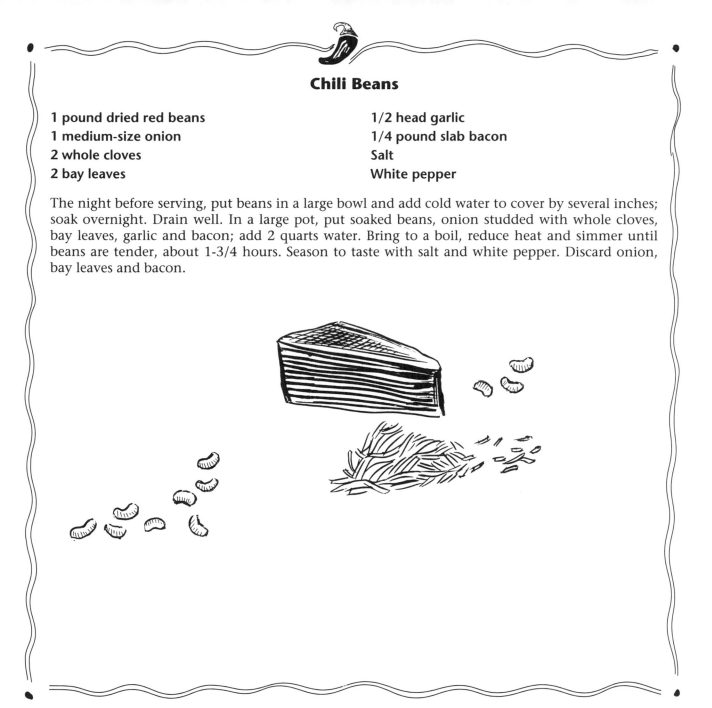

Caucus Club Texas Chili

Arthur Calloway, Caucus Club, Detroit, Michigan

Detroit's venerable Caucus Club has a quiet-but-devoted following for its good, meaty chili—the recipe for which was very kindly supplied by Chef Arthur Calloway. If you can't find powdered jalapeño chile, substitute an equivalent amount, or to taste, of very finely chopped fresh jalapeño—minus the seeds.

1 tablespoon bacon drippings

1 pound pork, cut into 1/2-inch cubes

3 pounds beef, cut into 1/2-inch cubes

1 medium-size onion, finely chopped

1 red bell pepper, cut into 1/4-inch dice

1 medium-size garlic clove, finely chopped

1 bay leaf

3 tablespoons chili powder

2 tablespoons ground cumin

2 teaspoons salt

1 teaspoon black pepper

1 teaspoon red (cayenne) pepper

1/2 teaspoon pure jalapeño (hot) chile powder

2 cups cooked kidney beans

1-1/2 cups water

3 tablespoons tomato paste

4 medium-size tomatoes, finely chopped (2 cups)

2 ounces white Cheddar cheese (1/2 cup), finely shredded, for garnish

2 medium-size Haas avocados, halved and cut lengthwise into thin slices, for garnish

3 medium-size green onions, white parts only, thinly sliced crosswise, for garnish

In a large pot, melt bacon drippings over medium heat. Add pork and sauté 15 minutes; add beef and sauté about 20 minutes more. Add onion and sauté until transparent, 5 to 7 minutes. Add bell pepper, garlic, bay leaf, chili powder, cumin, salt, pepper, cayenne and jalapeño chile powder. Cover and simmer 20 minutes. Add beans, water, tomato paste and tomatoes. Cover and simmer 45 minutes more. Serve in bowls, garnished with cheese, avocado slices and sliced green onions. Makes 10 servings.

Grilled Rabbit Chili

Gethin DuValle Thomas, Adirondacks, Washington, D.C.

Adirondacks, brainchild of restauranteur Michael McCarty, is one of the most vibrant parts of the recently restored Union Station in Washington, D.C.—not least for the innovative cuisine of chef Gethin Thomas. His version of chili takes the nouvelle approach of making it a spicy sauce for quickly grilled rabbit loins. If you'd prefer to use another meat, boneless and skinless chicken breasts would do nicely.

3 tablespoons sesame seeds

1/4 cup olive oil

4 garlic cloves, finely chopped

1/2 medium-size onion, finely chopped (1/3 cup)

2 tablespoons shelled pumpkin seeds

2 cups chicken broth

1/2 pound tomatoes, coarsely chopped

1 medium-size tomatillo (about 2 oz.), coarsely chopped

2 or 3 jalapeño chiles, stemmed, seeded and coarsely chopped

1 dried pasilla chile, stemmed

Salt and freshly ground black pepper

4 trimmed rabbit loins (6 to 8 ounces each)

In a small, ungreased skillet over medium heat, toast 1 tablespoon of the sesame seeds until light golden in color, 1 to 2 minutes; set aside. In a large skillet over medium-high heat, heat half of the oil. Add garlic, onion, pumpkin seeds and remaining sesame seeds; sauté until golden, 3 to 5 minutes. Add broth, tomatoes, tomatillo and chiles; bring to a boil, then reduce heat and simmer 20 minutes. Meanwhile, preheat grill or broiler. In a blender or food processor fitted with the metal blade, carefully process chile mixture until pureed; pass through a fine strainer, season to taste with salt and pepper and keep warm. Brush rabbit loins with remaining oil and season with pepper. Grill until medium done, about 3 minutes per side. Spoon chili sauce onto 4 serving plates. With a sharp knife, cut each loin at a 45-degree angle into slices about 1/2 inch thick. Fan sliced loin across each plate and garnish with reserved sesame seeds. Makes 4 servings.

Border Grill Vegetarian Red Bean Stew

Susan Feniger and Mary Sue Milliken, Border Grill, Santa Monica, California

At their Border Grill restaurants near the beach in Santa Monica and on L.A.'s trendy Melrose Avenue, owner/chefs Susan Feniger and Mary Sue Milliken manage the remarkable feat of offering Southwestern food that seems at once both authentically traditional and refreshingly modern. This rustic vegetarian chili is a fine example of how honest and direct their cooking is. They point out that, if you can find them in a local ethnic market, the best dried red beans come from El Salvador, and are prized for their small size, smooth skins and even color.

2 cups dried red beans, soaked overnight in cold water and drained

10 cups water

2 carrots, cut into large chunks

2 celery stalks, cut into large chunks

2 turnips, cut into large chunks

2 parsnips, cut into large chunks

4 red rose potatoes, cut into halves

1 zucchini, cut into medium-size chunks

1 yellow crookneck squash, cut into medium-size chunks

3/4 cup extra-virgin olive oil

4 large onions, finely chopped (4 cups)

Salt

Freshly ground black pepper

8 to 10 medium-size garlic cloves, finely chopped (4 tablespoons)

1 to 2 fresh ancho chiles, stemmed and seeded, then roasted (page 3) and pureed in a blender or food processor (6 tablespoons)

Rinse beans and put in a large pot with 6 cups water. Bring to a boil and simmer until beans are plump and creamy but still whole, 2 to 3 hours. While beans are cooking, bring water to a boil in a medium-size pot and preheat the grill or broiler. One vegetable at a time, blanch carrots, celery, turnips and parsnips in boiling water, 2 to 3 minutes each, removing with a slotted spoon; set aside. Boil potato halves until tender, 10 to 15 minutes; set aside. Lightly brush zucchini and crookneck squash chunks with olive oil and grill until golden, 3 to 5 minutes per side; set aside. When beans are done, heat 1/4 cup of olive oil in a large, heavy-bottomed pot over medium heat. Add onions, salt and pepper and sauté until dark golden brown, 10 to 15 minutes. Add garlic and sauté until its aroma rises, 1 to 2 minutes. Stir in pureed ancho chile. Add cooked beans, reserved vegetables and remaining water. Bring to a boil, reduce heat, and simmer until beans are slightly gooey and vegetables are hot and cooked through, 5 to 10 minutes more. Ladle into serving bowls and garnish with a tablespoon of Ancho Chile Salsa (opposite) and a drizzle of extra-virgin olive oil. Makes 6 servings.

Border Grill Ancho Chile Salsa

**2 fresh ancho chiles, stemmed
and seeded**
1 cup orange juice

1/2 cup lime juice
1/2 cup grapefruit juice
1/2 tablespoon salt

Preheat oven to 400°F (205°C). Place chiles in a baking pan and roast until tender, taking care not to burn, 7 to 10 minutes. Let cool, then finely chop and combine with juices and salt.

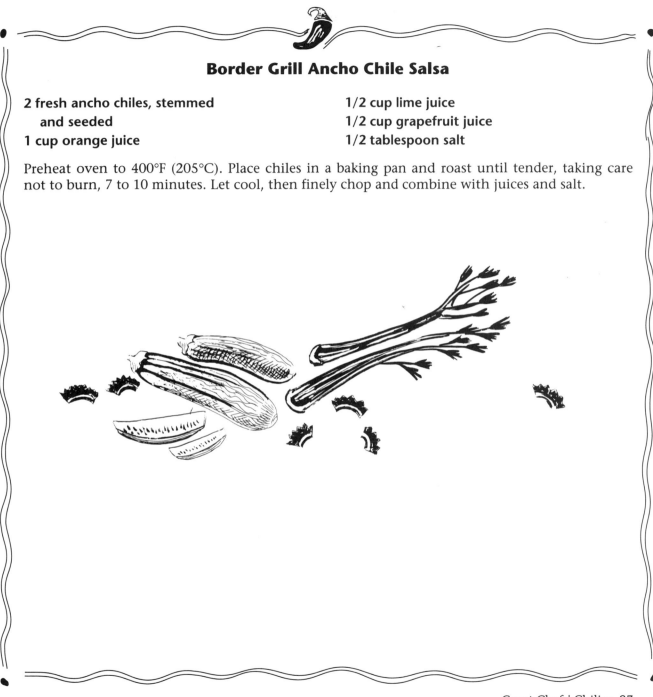

Bikini's Bowl of Green with Chilied Melon

John Sedlar, Bikini, Santa Monica, California

In the mid-1980s, John Sedlar captured the nation's attention with the Modern Southwest Cuisine he devised at Saint-Estephe, his restaurant in the Los Angeles beach community of Manhattan Beach. At his new restaurant, Bikini, Sedlar's wide-ranging international influences are more at the forefront, giving his creativity even freer rein, as can be seen in this unusual interpretation of chili—a green chile soup garnished with a refreshingly spicy melon mixture. As well as being a strikingly delicious combination, the two elements of this recipe are, I find, excellent on their own.

Chilied Melon (opposite)

2 tablespoons unsalted butter

2 medium-size russet potatoes, peeled and
   cut into 1/4-inch dice

12 fresh green Anaheim chiles, stemmed,
   seeded and coarsely chopped

2 medium-size onions, coarsely chopped

1 teaspoon dried leaf thyme

1 bay leaf

1 cup chicken broth

2 cups half-and-half

1 teaspoon salt

1 teaspoon white pepper

Prepare Chilied Melon and refrigerate. In a medium-size saucepan, melt half the butter over medium-high heat. Add potatoes and sauté about 5 minutes. Add chiles, onions, thyme and bay leaf and sauté about 2 minutes more. Add chicken broth. Bring to a boil, then reduce heat and simmer, uncovered, until vegetables are tender, about 25 minutes. Discard bay leaf. In a blender or food processor fitted with the metal blade, in batches if necessary, pour contents of pan, half-and-half, salt, pepper and remaining butter, and puree. Pass through a fine sieve. Return to pan and gently rewarm. Ladle into serving bowls and add a generous dollop of Chilied Melon in center. Makes 4 servings.

Chilied Melon

2 firm, ripe, sweet honeydew melons or
    cantaloupes, or 1 of each, peeled, seeded
    and cut into 1/4- to 1/2-inch cubes
1 tablespoon medium-hot pure chile powder
1 teaspoon dried red chile flakes

1 garlic clove, finely chopped
Juice of 3 limes
Salt
Freshly ground black pepper

In a medium-size bowl, combine melon, chile powder, chile flakes, garlic and lime juice. Season to taste with salt and pepper. Cover and refrigerate until serving.

Muscovy Duck Chili

Jody Denton, Eureka, Los Angeles, California

One of the hippest restaurants in L.A. these days is the brew pub Eureka, the latest success of Wolfgang Puck and his wife/colleague Barbara Lazaroff. Chef Jody Denton, in charge of the kitchen there, concocts wonderfully casual and exciting food to go with the fresh-brewed beers, and one dish that has won especially high critical raves is this particular chili. As the title suggests, they use Muscovy duck, which has a wonderfully rich and meaty flavor; but you could use whatever kind of duck meat is most readily available.

1/4 cup vegetable oil

5 pounds boneless, skinless duck meat, cut into 1/4- to 1/2-inch pieces

2 medium-size onions, finely chopped

8 to 10 garlic cloves, finely chopped (3 tablespoons)

2 dried pasilla chiles, toasted 1 to 2 minutes, stemmed, seeded (page 4) and coarsely chopped

3 tablespoons ground cumin

3 tablespoons freshly ground black pepper

3 tablespoons paprika

2 teaspoons ground cinnamon

1/2 cup tomato paste

3 large tomatoes, coarsely chopped

3 (12-oz.) bottles dark Mexican beer

2 quarts cooking liquid reserved from Black Beans & Canadian Bacon (page 105)

2 cups veal or duck stock

3 fresh serrano chiles, stemmed and finely chopped

2 fresh jalapeño chiles, stemmed and finely chopped

1 fresh jalapeño chile, stemmed, seeded and finely chopped

2 lemons, juiced, zests finely grated

1 cup finely chopped fresh cilantro

1/4 cup finely chopped fresh oregano

2 tablespoons finely chopped fresh thyme

6 cups cooked black beans

Salt

In a large skillet, heat just enough oil to coat over very high heat. Add duck in batches, sautéing until evenly seared, 1 to 2 minutes per batch, adding a little more oil if necessary. Set meat aside. In a large pot, heat just enough oil to coat the bottom over high heat. Add onions and sauté until lightly browned, 3 to 5 minutes. Add garlic, pasilla chiles, cumin, pepper, paprika and cinnamon; sauté 2 to 3 minutes more. Add tomato paste and sauté 2 to 3 minutes more, taking care to scrape bottom of pot to prevent burning. Add tomatoes, beer, bean liquid and stock; bring to a boil, reduce heat to low, and simmer 1-1/2 to 2 hours, stirring occasionally. Stir in remaining ingredients and serve. Makes 14 to 16 servings.

CHILI EMBELLISHMENTS

6

To many lovers of chili, the dish is essentially nothing more than an embellishment to another, more elaborate preparation. It's the thick, spicy topping to their favorite sandwich—a chili dog or chili burger, or the bun-less burger-and-chili diner classic known as the chili size.

To others, chili is the spice that gives life to Southwestern or Mexican favorites. You'll find it here holding together a heap of crisp tortilla chips in a plate of nachos; filling a flour tortilla burrito; and even ladled over a favorite brand of corn chips in an after-school favorite from Santa Fe, New Mexico.

Still other people manage to elaborate their chili while keeping it as the featured player. Guidelines in this chapter for making chili-topped spaghetti and a fanciful chili sundae admirably suit the needs of such aficionados.

And every one of these recipes is dedicated to those imaginative gourmets whose credo might be summed up thusly: "Never leave well enough alone!"

Classic Chili Dog

Here are the proportions and guidelines for a well-balanced, truly classic, all-American sandwich. Of course, you can make this with packaged commercial hot dogs and white buns. But that would defeat the fun of a really great chili dog: the snap and spice of a great deli-bought Vienna-style sausage, the slight chewiness of a good bakery roll, both complemented by generous spoonfuls of a really good, thick chili. My favorite candidates for the topping are the Chili Dog Chili on page 17, the Black Bean Chili Primavera on page 69 or the Black Bean & Canadian Bacon on page 105. But feel free to substitute any other thick-bodied chili that strikes your fancy.

1 (1/4-pound) Vienna-style sausage
1 bakery-style hot dog roll (onion roll
   optional)
Whole-grain Dijon-style mustard
1/4 to 1/3 cup chili, warmed

1/2 ounce sharp Cheddar cheese, coarsely
   shredded (2 tablespoons)
1 to 1-1/2 tablespoons finely chopped
   red onion

Put sausage in a saucepan of cold water, cover and place over medium heat. Put roll in oven and set oven to 350°F (175°C). When water reaches a full boil, drain sausage well. Slice halfway through warmed roll and put sausage inside. Spread generously with mustard. Spoon hot chili over sausage, sprinkle with cheese, add onions to taste and eat immediately. Makes 1 serving.

Chili Burger with Green Chiles

A classic chili burger gets extra zing from the addition of whole canned mild green chiles nestled between the burger and the melted cheese. If you really want to go wild, substitute a pepper Monterey Jack cheese—which includes flakes of hot chile right in the cheese—for the plain Monterey Jack, Cheddar or Swiss. Use one of the same selection of chilies suggested for the Chili Dog (opposite), or whichever chili—freshly made or canned—strikes your fancy.

1 freshly baked hamburger bun
6 ounces lean ground beef
1 (1/4-inch-thick) onion slice
1 tablespoon melted butter
Salt
Freshly ground black pepper

1 whole canned mild green chili, seeded
1 ounce sharp Cheddar, Monterey Jack or
   Swiss cheese, coarsely shredded (1/4 cup)
1/4 to 1/3 cup chili, warmed
Bottled chili sauce and ketchup

Preheat the broiler. Put bun in oven and set oven to 350°F (175°C). Form meat into a patty about 3/4 inch thick. Brush onion slice with butter. Season patty and onion on both sides with salt and pepper. Broil until patty is done to a little rarer than to taste and onion is golden; leave broiler on. Drape chile over top of patty and top with cheese; return to broiler until cheese melts. Put patty on lower half of bun. Top with onion, then spoon warm chili on top. Serve with bottled chili sauce and ketchup. Makes 1 serving.

Up-to-Date Chili Size

In the late 1950s, when I was growing up in Los Angeles, it seemed that all the coffee shops had a chili size—a grilled beef patty, topped with chili, cheese and other embellishments—on the menu. It was one of my favorites then, and it still is today. But now, rather than making it with a meaty chili, I prefer to make chili sizes with a vegetarian, bean chili topping such as those found in the Vegetable Chilies Chapter; and I add a little something extra, in the form of chopped mild green chiles in the burger and a few extra toppings. If you're so inclined, you could also substitute ground turkey for the beef. I've given quantities for one serving here, but the recipe is easily expandable.

6 ounces lean ground beef
1 tablespoon finely chopped canned
   mild green chiles
Salt
Freshly ground black pepper
3/4 cup cooked chili, warmed

1 ounce sharp Cheddar cheese, coarsely
   shredded (1/4 cup)
1 tablespoon dairy sour cream
1 tablespoon finely chopped red onion
1 tablespoon finely chopped fresh cilantro
2 or 3 pitted ripe olives, thinly sliced
Bottled chili sauce and ketchup

Preheat the broiler. In a small bowl, thoroughly mix together beef and chiles. Form a patty about 3/4 inch thick and season with salt and pepper. Broil until done to taste. Leave broiler on. Put cooked patty in a shallow individual-serving baking dish and smother with chili. Sprinkle cheese evenly on top and place under broiler until cheese is melted and bubbling. Top with sour cream, onion, cilantro and olives. Serve with bottled chili sauce and ketchup. Makes 1 serving.

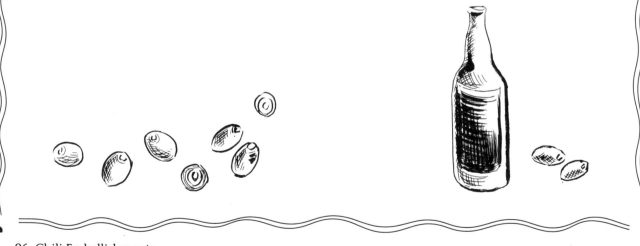

Deluxe Double-Chili Burritos

A large flour tortilla can, like a sort of little burro, carry quite a cargo of leftover chili—whichever you make from the meat, poultry and/or bean-based recipes in this book. Use large homemade (page 108) or store-bought tortillas for the wrappers. To give these burritos an extra-lavish twist, I've coated them with a New Mexican-style chili sauce—essentially your choice of the sauces on pages 23 or 24, made without the meat.

4 large flour tortillas
1/2 recipe homemade chili with meat, poultry and/or beans (about 3 cups)
6 ounces sharp Cheddar cheese, shredded (1-1/2 cups)
6 ounces Monterey Jack cheese, shredded (1-1/2 cups)
1 recipe Old-Fashioned New Mexican Red Chile or Old-Fashioned New Mexican Green Chile (pages 23 and 24), made without the meat; or 1/2 recipe made with the meat

6 tablespoons dairy sour cream
1/2 cup Guacamole (page 115)
16 pitted ripe olives, thinly sliced
6 large iceberg lettuce leaves, thinly shredded
4 Roma tomatoes, seeded and coarsely chopped

Preheat the broiler. Warm a heavy skillet over medium heat. One at a time, warm tortillas on skillet, about 30 seconds per side. Place tortillas on a work surface and spoon chili evenly among them, spreading it evenly in center of each tortilla. Sprinkle half of Cheddar and Jack cheeses evenly over chili. Fold in 2 sides of each tortilla about 2 inches. Fold up bottom of tortilla over filling, then roll up tortilla to form a cylinder. Place each burrito, flap down, in the center of a broilerproof serving plate. Spoon New Mexican red or green chile over and around each burrito. Sprinkle remaining cheese on top of burritos. Put burritos under hot broiler just until cheese melts and begins to bubble. Place a dollop of sour cream on center of each burrito, and dollops of guacamole on either side. Scatter sour cream and guacamole with olives. Arrange lettuce around each burrito and scatter tomatoes all over each plate. Makes 4 servings.

Chili Nachos

You can bring greater distinction to one of the most popular, casual Mexican appetizers by making your own crisp tortilla chips or Tostaditas (page 00), and topping them with your favorite homemade chili instead of the usual paste of refried beans. Since only a cup of chili is needed, it's a great way to use up leftovers. Though in most cases you'll want to try it with one of the basics, like Chili Dog Chili (page 17) or Quick Beef & Bacon Chili & Beans (page 18), there's no reason you couldn't go fancier with whatever chili you happen to have around.

1 recipe Tostaditas (page 107)
1 cup leftover cooked chili, warmed
3 ounces sharp Cheddar cheese, shredded
   (3/4 cup)
3 ounces Monterey Jack cheese, shredded
   (3/4 cup)
3 tablespoons dairy sour cream

1/4 cup Guacamole (page 115)
4 large iceberg lettuce leaves, thinly
   shredded
2 medium-size Roma tomatoes, coarsely
   chopped
8 pitted ripe olives, thinly sliced

Preheat the broiler, with rack 8 to 10 inches from heat. Arrange half the Tostaditas on a broiler-proof serving plate, with corners pointing upward. Spoon half the chili over chips and sprinkle evenly with about a third of the cheeses. Arrange remaining Tostaditas on top. Spoon remaining chili and scatter remaining cheese over them. Broil until cheese melts and begins to bubble, 3 to 5 minutes, keeping close watch to make sure that tostaditas do not burn. Place sour cream in center of nachos, with dollops of guacamole on either side. Arrange lettuce around rim and scatter tomato and olives over center. Let guests help themselves from plate. Makes 4 servings.

Frito Pie

I first heard about this legendary treat from my good friend John Sedlar, owner/chef of Saint-Estephe and Bikini restaurants in Los Angeles, who grew up in Santa Fe, New Mexico, and observed—first-hand—this nachos-style dish—a specialty of the Woolworth's store just off the Plaza there. They actually serve it in the Fritos® bag, slitting open the side and ladling in the chili. In my own elaboration of that basic idea, I suggest serving it in a shallow bowl, as described below. Use a fairly simple chili recipe for your topping—such as the Chili Dog Chili (page 17), Old Fashioned New Mexican Red Chile with Beef (page 23) or Hearty Ground Turkey Chili (page 43). You can even use your favorite canned chili, as they do for authentic Frito Pies—though far be it from me to steer you in that direction!

4 cups Fritos®-brand corn chips
4 cups cooked chili, warmed

1/4 pound sharp Cheddar cheese, shredded
(1 cup)
1 small onion, finely chopped

Distribute corn chips among 4 shallow serving bowls. Ladle chili over chips. Sprinkle with cheese and chopped onion to taste. Eat with a soup spoon. Makes 4 servings.

Chili Spaghetti

Here's a great way to use up some leftover chili: Serve it diner-style, over cooked spaghetti. The ones that work best with this kind of presentation are your basic meat or meat-and-bean chilies.

1 cup hot cooked spaghetti

1 cup cooked chili, warmed

2 tablespoons freshly grated Parmesan or Romano cheese

1 tablespoon finely chopped red onion, for garnish

1 tablespoon finely chopped fresh Italian parsley, for garnish

Put spaghetti in a shallow serving bowl, and top with chili. Sprinkle generously with cheese, and garnish with red onion and parsley. Makes 1 serving.

Chili Sundae

A fanciful creation of the all-American diner, this chili embellishment is a sort of culinary trompe l'oeil: *Making a serving of chili resemble a soda fountain treat in a traditional, fluted ice cream sundae glass. While most chili sundaes are straight chili with toppings, I've furthered the illusion here by serving the chili atop mashed potatoes—just as you'd serve a sauce on top of ice cream. If you want to enhance the fantasy even more, search your supermarket for a jar of little cherry-tomato-size pickled red chiles, to impersonate maraschino cherries.*

3/4 cup freshly mashed potatoes
3/4 cup cooked chili, warmed
**1/2 ounce sharp Cheddar cheese, cut into
   small dice**

**2 tablespoons dairy sour cream, lightly
   whipped with a fork**
1 pickled red "cherry" chile, for garnish

With an ice cream scoop, place 2 generous balls of hot mashed potatoes into a fluted sundae dish large enough to hold both potatoes and chili. Ladle chili on top. Sprinkle with cheese. Spoon a generous dollop of sour cream on top to resemble whipped cream. Garnish with pickled chile. Makes 1 serving.

CHILI COMPANIONS

7

A bowl of chili may well be the main attraction of a satisfying, exciting meal. But man and woman do not live by chili alone. This chapter features some traditional—and not-so-traditional— recipes that happily accompany chili.

It begins with starchy dishes—more commonly called complex carbohydrates today—that are not only filling but also offset somewhat the heat of a bowl of chili. Traditional bean dishes are appropriate in this role when serving chilies in which no beans are included. Rice—in this case, a nicely seasoned version of Spanish rice—also does the job well. So too do cornmeal and wheat, in the form of tamales, tortillas, corn breads and muffins. I've also included a recipe for crisp potato skins, which can elevate chili into a fashionable hors d'oeuvre.

Fresh vegetables provide a cooling contrast to chili. You'll find them here in a tomato salsa, a creamy guacamole and a tangy coleslaw. In addition, there's a recipe for an unusual, refreshing combination: the salad of oranges and red onions known as Pico de Gallo.

One final matter to be dealt with, of course, is the powerful thirst a bowl of chili can create. The three traditional cooling cocktails included here ably do their part in helping to put out the fire.

Robust Boiled Beans

To balance a fiery chili in which no beans are present, this satisfying side dish is deliberately spice-free—apart from the cumin, which serves to enhance the beans' earthy flavor. It's worth boiling up at least a pound of dried beans, since they take a few hours to simmer and they freeze very well. If you like, you can add a smoked ham hock for some extra flavor, though the taste is perfectly satisfying if you follow the vegetarian version below.

1 pound dried red beans or pinto beans	2 medium-size onions, finely chopped
2 bay leaves	2 teaspoons ground cumin
3 tablespoons olive oil	2 teaspoons salt
2 medium-size garlic cloves, finely chopped	1 teaspoon white pepper

In a large pot, put beans with enough cold water to cover by several inches. Bring to a boil, boil 5 minutes, then remove from heat and let soak 1 hour. Drain well and rinse. Return beans to pot with bay leaves and enough fresh water to cover. Bring to a boil, then reduce heat and simmer, adding water as necessary to keep beans covered, until beans are very tender, 2 to 3 hours. In a skillet, heat oil over medium heat. Add garlic and onions and sauté until they just begin to turn golden, 5 to 7 minutes. Add cumin and sauté 1 minute more. Stir mixture into beans with salt and pepper and continue simmering gently until beans are thick, with no excess liquid above them, 15 to 30 minutes more. Discard bay leaves. Makes about 7 cups, 14 side-dish servings.

Black Beans & Canadian Bacon

Black beans may well have the richest, earthiest flavor of all dried beans, which is beautifully complemented by the smoky taste of a little Canadian bacon in this rich and savory side dish. Canadian bacon, incidentally, is usually very lean, so you're getting its culinary benefits at a fairly low dietary cost!

1 pound dried black beans
4 medium-size garlic cloves, left whole and
   unpeeled
2 medium-size onions, cut in halves
2 bay leaves

1 teaspoon ground cumin
1/2 pound Canadian bacon, cut into
   1/4-inch dice
2 teaspoons salt
3/4 teaspoon freshly ground black pepper

In a large pot, put beans with enough cold water to cover by several inches. Bring to a boil, boil for 5 minutes, then remove from heat and let soak 1 hour. Drain well and rinse. Return beans to pot with garlic, onions, bay leaves, cumin and enough fresh water to cover. Bring to a boil, then reduce heat and simmer, adding water as necessary to keep beans covered, until beans are very tender, 2 to 3 hours. Stir in bacon, salt and pepper and simmer until beans are thick, with no excess liquid above them, 15 to 30 minutes more. Remove and discard onion halves, bay leaves and garlic cloves. Makes about 7 cups, 14 side-dish servings.

Spanish Chile Rice

This version of Spanish rice gets an extra hint of spiciness—still well within the tolerance range of most palates—from the inclusion of a fresh green Anaheim chile and from the use of canned spicy tomato juice as part of its cooking liquid. Serve alongside, or as a base for, your favorite chili.

2 tablespoons olive oil
1 fresh green Anaheim chile, stemmed,
   seeded and cut into 1/4-inch dice
1/2 small red onion, cut into 1/4-inch dice

1/2 cup water
2 (6-oz.) cans spicy tomato juice
1 cup long-grain white rice
1 teaspoon salt

In a medium-size saucepan, heat oil over medium heat. Add chile and onion and sauté until onion is transparent, 1 to 2 minutes. Add water and tomato juice, increase heat and bring to a boil. Add rice and salt, reduce heat, cover and simmer gently until rice is tender, about 20 minutes. Before serving, stir lightly with a fork to fluff rice and combine ingredients. Makes 6 servings.

Double-Green Tamales

Essentially cornmeal dumplings steamed in corn husks, tamales make a wonderfully flavorful starchy accompaniment to chili—whether they're served on the side or have the chili ladled over them. This version gets its name because the tamales include both fresh corn—often known as "green corn" when used in tamales—and canned green mild chiles. If fresh corn is out of season, you may substitute canned. Dried corn husks are available in the ethnic food sections of well-stocked supermarkets, or in Latino groceries; if you can't find them, wrap the tamales in heavy-duty foil or plastic wrap, securing them with kitchen string.

14 large dried corn husks
2 cups masa harina
1/2 tablespoon salt
1/2 tablespoon sugar
1-1/4 teaspoons baking powder
1/3 cup vegetable shortening
3 tablespoons unsalted butter, softened

1 cup milk
2 small ears fresh corn, kernels removed
 (3/4 to 1 cup)
1 whole canned mild green chile, cut into
 strips about 2" x 1/4"
1-1/2 ounces Monterey Jack cheese, shredded
 (6 tablespoons)

In the sink or a large bowl, put corn husks and enough lukewarm water to cover. Soak about 5 minutes. Meanwhile, in a medium-size bowl or a food processor fitted with the metal blade, combine masa, salt, sugar and baking powder. Add shortening and butter and mash with a pastry cutter or a fork, or by pulsing processor, until mixture resembles fine crumbs. Add milk and stir or process to form a soft paste. Stir in corn kernels. Drain corn husks and tear 2 lengthwise into 1/4- to 1/2-inch-wide strips. In center of a whole corn husk, place 2 tablespoons tamale mixture, spreading to form rectangle about 1/2 inch thick and 3" x 1". Sprinkle a little cheese and some chile strips in center of rectangle. Top with 2 tablespoons more tamale mixture, patting edges to enclose cheese and chiles. Fold up top and bottom of corn husk, then fold in sides, to enclose tamale completely; tie securely across middle with strip of corn husk. Repeat with remaining husks and ingredients. In a vegetable steamer, bring several inches of water to a boil. Place tamales in a steamer basket, cover and cook about 45 minutes. Remove from steamer and let cool about 5 minutes before serving and letting guests unwrap individual portions. Makes 12 tamales, 6 servings.

Homemade Corn Tortillas

It's surprising how easily tortillas can be made at home. Special ground corn—masa harina—is available in most supermarkets. To shape the tortillas, you might want to try patting balls of dough back and forth between your hands, like some Mexican women do. Or you could use a cast-iron tortilla press. Or just put each ball of dough between two sheets of waxed paper or heavy-duty plastic wrap and roll with a rolling pin.

2 cups masa harina
1/4 teaspoon salt

1 to 1-1/4 cups warm water

In a medium-size bowl, stir together masa and salt. Stir in enough water to make a thick, firm, but still soft dough. Heat a cast-iron griddle or heavy skillet over medium-high heat. Divide dough into 12 equal balls. One at a time, roll or press a ball into a tortilla roughly 6 inches in diameter. Place tortilla on hot griddle and cook until it just begins to turn golden and its edges curl, 1 to 1-1/2 minutes per side. Transfer to a napkin-lined basket while preparing remainder. Makes 12.

Tostaditas

More commonly known as taco chips, these snacks are excellent dipped into, crumbled over, or munched alongside a bowl of your favorite chili—or as the base for a platter of Chili Nachos (page 98). You can make them with store-bought corn tortillas; but they're especially flavorful fried up from a homemade batch. If you increase the recipe size, be extra-sure to fry in batches so you don't wind up with greasy, not-quite-crisp chips. For a refreshing change, try a spritz of fresh lime juice over the just-fried chips.

Vegetable oil for deep-frying
8 corn tortillas, cut into 6 wedges each

Salt
Fresh lime wedges (optional)

In a large, heavy skillet or deep-fryer, heat 2 to 3 inches of oil to 360°F (185°C) on a deep-frying thermometer, or until a scrap of tortilla sizzles briskly when dropped in. Without overcrowding skillet, cook tortilla wedges in batches until crisp and deep golden-brown, 2 to 3 minutes. Remove with a wire skimmer and drain well on paper towels. Season to taste with salt and, if you like, a squeeze of lime. Makes 4 servings.

Homemade Flour Tortillas

Freshly made and hot, these soft, thin Mexican flatbreads are terrific alongside a bowl of chili. They're also great filled with chili to make a burrito (page 97). If you make a big batch, stack the cooked tortillas and seal in an airtight plastic bag, where they'll keep well for several days in the refrigerator or several weeks in the freezer. To reheat, wrap in foil and warm in a 400°F (205°C) oven 5 to 10 minutes.

2 cups all-purpose flour
1 teaspoon baking powder
1 teaspoon sugar
1 teaspoon salt

1/3 cup vegetable shortening
1/2 cup water
1/4 cup milk

In a medium-size bowl, stir together flour, baking powder, sugar and salt. Make a well in the center of flour mixture. Add shortening. With your fingertips, rub together flour and shortening until mixture is evenly combined and resembles coarse crumbs. In a measuring cup, combine water and milk. Make well again in flour mixture, add 1/2 cup of liquid, and stir with a fork to combine, adding enough extra liquid as necessary to make a soft dough. Turn dough out onto a floured surface and knead about 5 minutes. Return to bowl, cover with plastic wrap and let rest at room temperature about 30 minutes. Heat a cast-iron griddle or heavy skillet over medium heat. On floured surface, divide dough into 12 equal balls; toss balls with flour to coat, and return to covered bowl. One at a time roll out each ball into a thin tortilla 8 to 10 inches in diameter. Place tortilla immediately on hot griddle and cook until its surface appears dry and speckled with brown spots, about 1 minute per side. Transfer to a napkin-lined basket while preparing remainder. Makes 12.

Goat Cheese, Tomato & Cilantro Quesadillas

While you can use any favorite cheese to fill these griddle-cooked flour tortillas, I find a fresh, creamy goat cheese an especially flavorful addition—and a nice, slightly tangy contrast to the flavor of a well-spiced chili.

6 store-bought or Homemade Flour Tortillas
  (opposite)
1/4 pound fresh creamy goat cheese
3 ounces Monterey Jack cheese, shredded
  (3/4 cup)

2 firm ripe Roma tomatoes, seeded and cut
  into 1/4-inch dice
6 tablespoons finely chopped fresh cilantro

Preheat a cast-iron griddle or heavy skillet over medium heat. Place tortillas on a work surface. With a knife, evenly spread goat cheese across half of each tortilla's surface. Evenly sprinkle Jack cheese on top of goat cheese. Sprinkle tomato and cilantro evenly over cheeses. Fold other sides of tortillas over filling to form half-circles. Cook filled tortillas on griddle until hot and golden brown, 2 to 3 minutes per side. Transfer to cutting board and, with a heavy knife, cut each into 4 to 6 wedges and carefully transfer to serving plates with knife blade or a spatula. Makes 6 servings.

Honey-Cinnamon Sopaipillas

These little pastry-like pillows of dough—half way between a fry bread and a pastry—are a favorite accompaniment to spicy main courses in New Mexico. I've added just a hint of cinnamon and honey to make them extra delicious.

1 cup milk
2 tablespoons honey
2-1/2 cups all-purpose flour
2 tablespoons baking powder

1 teaspoon ground cinnamon
1 teaspoon salt
1/4 cup vegetable shortening
Vegetable oil for deep-frying

In a small saucepan over medium-low heat, warm milk and honey, stirring frequently, until honey has dissolved. Set aside. In a medium-size bowl, stir together flour, baking powder, cinnamon and salt. With your fingers, rub shortening into dry ingredients. Add warm milk and stir with a fork just until a soft, moist dough forms; do not over mix. Turn dough out onto a floured surface and knead gently until smooth, 3 to 4 minutes at most. Return to bowl, cover with plastic wrap and let rest about 30 minutes. Divide dough into 2 equal portions. On floured surface, roll each into a long cylinder about 1 inch in diameter. With a rolling pin, roll each cylinder to form an even rectangle about 3 inches wide and 1/4 inch thick. Cut rectangles into triangles with three equal sides about 4 inches long. Stack triangles in single layers between waxed paper. In a large, deep, heavy skillet or deep-fryer, heat 2 to 3 inches of oil to 375°F (190°C) on a deep-frying thermometer. Fry several triangles at a time, without crowding, turning them once and keeping them covered by pushing down with a wire skimmer or slotted spoon, until golden brown, about 1-1/2 minutes. Remove with skimmer and drain on paper towels. Repeat with remaining batches. Serve hot. Makes about 24 sopaipillas, 6 servings.

Piñon-Honey Corn Bread

Traditional corn bread gets a Southwestern twist with the addition of piñones—*pine nuts to those of us who don't live in those parts—and honey.*

1 cup yellow cornmeal
1 cup all-purpose flour
1 cup pine nuts (*piñones*)
1-1/2 tablespoons baking powder
1 teaspoon salt

1 cup milk
6 tablespoons unsalted butter, melted
1 egg, lightly beaten
1/4 cup honey, at room temperature

Preheat oven to 400°F (205°C). Lightly grease an 8-inch square baking pan. In a medium-size bowl, combine cornmeal, flour, pine nuts, baking powder and salt. In a separate bowl, stir together milk, butter and egg. Add to dry ingredients with honey and stir just until combined. Spoon batter into prepared baking pan and bake until golden and a cake tester or wooden pick inserted into center comes out clean, about 25 minutes. Serve warm, cut into 4″ x 2″ pieces. Makes 8 servings.

Old Glory Corn Muffins

The colors of the flag fly stirringly in these moist and flavorful muffins: red bell pepper dice, white corn kernels and shreds of Monterey Jack cheese and blue cornmeal. There's also just the slightest hint of fireworks from red chile flakes, though overall the muffins make a palate-soothing accompaniment to a hearty bowl of chili. If you can't find blue cornmeal, by all means make the recipe with yellow.

1 cup blue cornmeal

1 cup all-purpose flour

6 tablespoons sugar

1-1/2 tablespoons baking powder

2 teaspoons dried red chile flakes

1 teaspoon salt

1/4 pound Monterey Jack cheese, coarsely
   shredded (1 cup)

1/2 cup canned white corn kernels, drained

1/2 medium-size red bell pepper, cut into
   1/4-inch dice

1-1/4 cups buttermilk

6 tablespoons unsalted butter, melted

1 egg, lightly beaten

Preheat oven to 375°F (190°C). Grease the cups of a 12-cup muffin pan. In a medium-size bowl, stir together cornmeal, flour, sugar, baking powder, chile flakes and salt. Add cheese, corn and bell pepper; stir lightly to combine. Add buttermilk, butter and egg and stir briefly to make an evenly moistened batter. Spoon generously into prepared muffin cups. Bake until golden-brown, 25 to 30 minutes. Makes 12 muffins.

Sourdough Parmesan Toasts

You'll find some version of these easily made, crisp and savory toasts accompanying chili in many restaurants, both haughty and humble. They're really fun to dip into a thick bowlful. The recipe makes enough for a crowd—great for a casual chili party; but you can easily halve or quarter it. If you can't find a flute-shaped or other long, narrow sourdough loaf, uses slices from a larger loaf, cutting them in halves; or substitute regular, fine-crumbed French bread. The recipe works very well with bread that's a day or two old, whose drier texture stands up well to thin slicing.

1-1/2 cups (3/4 pound) unsalted butter, softened

6 ounces Parmesan cheese, finely grated (2 cups)

1 (12-inch-long) sourdough flute (3 to 4 inches in diameter), cut diagonally into 1/4-inch-thick slices

Preheat oven to 375°F (190°C). In a shallow bowl, use a fork to mash together butter and cheese until smoothly blended. Spread mixture generously on one side of each bread slice, placing slices side by side, buttered-side up, on baking sheets. Bake, in batches if necessary, until crisp and golden-brown, about 12 minutes. Serve immediately in a napkin-lined basket. Makes about 48 pieces.

Double-Baked Potato Skins

Spoon your favorite chili into these crisp potato shells and you've got a delightful appetizer, topped with shredded cheese, sour cream and chopped onion. Or just serve the skins as a side dish with a main course of chili. Unlike most potato skins, this recipe is not deep-fried. Rather, as the name suggests, the potatoes are first baked; then halved, hollowed out, brushed with olive oil and baked again until crisp. The results are lighter and, I think, much more delicious. For a crowd, this recipe very easily doubles, triples, quadruples or whatever.

4 medium-size russet potatoes, scrubbed well
  and dried
1/4 cup olive oil

Salt
White pepper

Rub potatoes with 1 tablespoon of the olive oil, reserving remaining 3 tablespoons. Put potatoes in a baking dish in a 400°F (205°C) oven. Bake until tender, 1 to 1-1/4 hours. When potatoes are cool enough to handle, cut each in half lengthwise. With a sharp-edged spoon, scoop out halves, reserving potato flesh for another use, leaving 1/4-inch-thick shells. Brush shells evenly with remaining oil and season to taste with salt and pepper. Return to baking dish and bake at 400°F (205°C) until crisp and golden-brown, about 45 minutes. Makes 4 servings.

Fresh Tomato Salsa

A dollop of this quickly prepared, Mexican-style table condiment adds extra flavor and zip to a bowl of chili. It's also great served as a dip with Tostaditas (page 107). Feel free to vary the quantities to your own taste, using more or less onion, jalapeño and cilantro as you like. Some people also prefer the extra-fresh flavor of the salsa just after it's made; others like it after the ingredients have had a chance to mingle awhile in the refrigerator. Try it both ways and decide for yourself!

1 pound firm ripe Roma tomatoes, seeded
  and cut into 1/4-inch pieces
1 fresh jalapeño chile, stemmed, seeded and
  very finely chopped
1/2 small red onion, finely chopped

2 tablespoons finely chopped fresh cilantro
2 teaspoons lemon juice
2 teaspoons red wine vinegar
1/2 teaspoon salt
1/2 teaspoon sugar

In a medium-size bowl, toss all ingredients together. Cover with plastic wrap and refrigerate until serving. Makes 2 generous cups.

Guacamole

The popular avocado dip makes a cooling side dish to a bowl of chili. Accompany with Tostaditas (page 107). For a more salad-like presentation, serve individual portions on beds of shredded romaine lettuce. The recipe may easily be doubled or tripled, as needed.

2 medium-size ripe Haas avocados
2 medium-size Roma tomatoes, seeded and
   cut into 1/4-inch dice
Juice of 1 small lime (about 2 tablespoons)
1/4 medium-size red onion, finely chopped
   (about 1/4 cup)

1/4 cup finely chopped canned mild green
   chiles
1 tablespoon finely chopped fresh cilantro
1/2 teaspoon salt
1/2 teaspoon white pepper

Peel avocados and discard pits. In a medium-size bowl, coarsely mash the avocado with a fork. Stir in remaining ingredients until well blended. Serve immediately. Makes about 2 cups, 4 servings.

Orange & Red Onion Pico de Gallo

The Spanish name for this dish means "rooster's beak," referring no doubt to the sharp bite of both the orange and the onion. It's a surprisingly delicious combination, part salad and part condiment, that makes a wonderfully cooling companion to a bowl of chili.

4 large navel oranges
1 medium-size red onions, very thinly sliced
1/4 cup finely chopped fresh cilantro

1/2 teaspoon dried red chile flakes
1/2 teaspoon salt

With a paring knife, carefully remove peels from oranges, cutting thickly enough to also remove translucent outer membrane of fruit. Then, also with knife, carefully cut individual orange sections away from membranes. Place oranges in a medium-size bowl and squeeze juice from orange membranes over them. Add onions, cilantro, chile flakes and salt. Toss well, cover and refrigerate at least 1/2 hour before serving. Makes 6 to 8 servings.

Sour Cream-Lemon Slaw

Lighter and tangier than conventional mayonnaise-dressed slaws, this version features a simple dressing of sour cream and lemon juice that helps make it a refreshing side dish to hot chili. If you like the slaw extra crisp, as I do, mix it up shortly before serving; for a more limp slaw, prepare an hour or two in advance and refrigerate, covered. I find this recipe even easier to prepare if you buy the bags of pre-shredded cabbage sold in many supermarket produce sections.

3/4 pound white cabbage, finely shredded
1 small carrot, finely shredded
1/4 cup finely chopped parsley
1 cup dairy sour cream
1/4 cup lemon juice

2 teaspoons sugar
1 teaspoon celery seeds
1/2 teaspoon white pepper
1/4 teaspoon salt

In a large bowl, toss together cabbage, carrot and parsley. In a separate bowl, stir together remaining ingredients. Pour dressing mixture over cabbage and toss well. Makes 6 to 8 servings.

Triple-Citrus Margaritas

This ultra fresh-tasting version of the classic cocktail makes a hot bowl of chili go down mighty easily. If you're serving these to guests, though, make sure there's a designated driver! In these health-conscious times, the salt-rimmed glasses are optional.

1/2 fresh lime
Salt
1 cup gold tequila
1/4 cup triple sec

2 tablespoons fresh orange juice
2 tablespoons fresh lemon juice
2 tablespoons fresh lime juice

Rub the rims of 4 cocktail or flat champagne glasses with cut side of lime half. Pour small pile of salt on a plate and dip moistened glass rims in salt to coat. Fill a cocktail shaker with ice. Add tequila, triple sec and citrus juices. Shake well and strain into prepared glasses. Makes 4 servings.

Fresh Pineapple Piña Coladas

There's something very soothing about sipping a piña colada while eating hot chili. Give these a try—but be very careful of the punch they pack!

3/4 cup pineapple juice
1/2 cup rum
1/2 cup fresh pineapple, cut into 1/2-inch
   chunks

1/2 cup canned cream of coconut
4 ice cubes

Put all ingredients in a blender. Blend until pineapple and ice are completely liquified and drink is smooth. Pour into chilled highball glasses. Makes 4 servings.

Jalapeño Bloody Marias

Tequila and a pickled jalapeño chile gives this Latinized version of a bloody Mary extra kick and tang. Be sure to plan in advance that at least one member of your dinner party is teetotalling it.

1-1/2 cups good-quality tomato juice, chilled
1 whole pickled jalapeño chile, stemmed and
   seeded
3/4 cup tequila, chilled

1/4 cup lemon juice
1 teaspoon Tabasco sauce
1/2 teaspoon celery salt

In a blender, put 1/2 cup of tomato juice and jalapeño chile. Process until chile is pureed. Fill a cocktail shaker with ice and add tomato-jalapeño mixture and remaining ingredients. Shake well and strain into highball glasses filled with ice. Makes 4 servings.

INDEX

Comparison to Metric Measure

When You Know	Symbol	Multiply By	To Find	Symbol
teaspoons	tsp	5.0	milliliters	ml
tablespoons	tbsp	15.0	milliliters	ml
fluid ounces	fl. oz.	30.0	milliliters	ml
cups	c	0.24	liters	l
pints	pt.	0.47	liters	l
quarts	qt.	0.95	liters	l
ounces	oz.	28.0	grams	g
pounds	lb.	0.45	kilograms	kg
Fahrenheit	F	5/9 (after subtracting 32)	Celsius	C

Liquid Measure to Milliliters

1/4 teaspoon	=	1.25 milliliters
1/2 teaspoon	=	2.5 milliliters
3/4 teaspoon	=	3.75 milliliters
1 teaspoon	=	5.0 milliliters
1-1/4 teaspoons	=	6.25 milliliters
1-1/2 teaspoons	=	7.5 milliliters
1-3/4 teaspoons	=	8.75 milliliters
2 teaspoons	=	10.0 milliliters
1 tablespoon	=	15.0 milliliters
2 tablespoons	=	30.0 milliliters

Fahrenheit to Celsius

F	C
200–205	95
220–225	105
245–250	120
275	135
300–305	150
325–330	165
345–350	175
370–375	190
400–405	205
425–430	220
445–450	230
470–475	245
500	260

Liquid Measure to Liters

1/4 cup	=	0.06 liters
1/2 cup	=	0.12 liters
3/4 cup	=	0.18 liters
1 cup	=	0.24 liters
1-1/4 cups	=	0.3 liters
1-1/2 cups	=	0.36 liters
2 cups	=	0.48 liters
2-1/2 cups	=	0.6 liters
3 cups	=	0.72 liters
3-1/2 cups	=	0.84 liters
4 cups	=	0.96 liters
4-1/2 cups	=	1.08 liters
5 cups	=	1.2 liters
5-1/2 cups	=	1.32 liters

About the Author

Norman Kolpas, noted food expert, has written for *The Times* of London, the *International Herald Tribune* and numerous magazines. He is the author of several books, including: *Breakfast and Brunch Book, Hors d'Oeuvres, Sweet Indulgences, Pasta Presto, Pasta Light, Pizza California Style, The Bel Air Book of Southern California Food and Entertaining, The Coffee Lover's Companion, The Chocolate Lover's Companion* and *The Gourmet's Lexicon*. Norman Kolpas lives in Los Angeles with his wife, novelist Katie Goldman, and his son Jacob.